Trusting God When
Our Children Die

Trusting God When Our Children Die

A Biblical Explanation of Why Children Are
Declared Innocent in the Judgment of God

ROBERT STEVEN HAYS SR.

WIPF & STOCK · Eugene, Oregon

TRUSTING GOD WHEN OUR CHILDREN DIE
A Biblical Explanation of Why Children Are Declared Innocent in the
Judgment of God

Wipf & Stock
An Imprint of Wipf and Stock Publishers
199 W. 8th Ave., Suite 3
Eugene, OR 97401

www.wipfandstock.com

PAPERBACK ISBN: 979-8-3852-1384-9
HARDCOVER ISBN: 979-8-3852-1385-6
EBOOK ISBN: 979-8-3852-1386-3

03/04/24

All Scripture quotations are taken from the King James Version. Any
deviation from that sacred text is unintentional.

Contents

Preface

THERE ARE MANY TRAGEDIES that we endure in this life, and one of them is the death of an innocent. These innocents are babies and young children, those born with mental disabilities, and those who acquired a mental disability at a young age which keeps them from understanding the natural law that God placed in every person (Rom 2:15). Parents are not supposed to have to bury their children; it should be the other way around. The tragedy of a baby or toddler dying is all too real and frequent. Birth defects also happen through no fault of any specific person other than Adam, and those with some birth defects never reach a mental capability of understanding.

The subject of the death of an innocent has been one I have dealt with several times as a pastor. I am not satisfied with standing in a pulpit and declaring a specific thing of which I do not necessarily have a firm belief. The reality of children dying requires the minister to offer help and comfort in a time of great need. I cannot offer that help or hope unless I am certain of it myself.

Death is Satan's weapon against mankind, and Christians need to have an answer for what happens beyond the physical life. Death is mankind's greatest fear. There is no excuse for the saints of God to not have an answer to the hope of life that we possess. First Peter 3:15: "But sanctify the Lord God in your hearts: and be ready always to give an answer to every man that asked you a reason of the hope that is in you with meekness and fear." We are given a Bible to "know" the answers, not just guess or hope for the best. First John 5:13: "These things have I written unto you that believe on the name of the Son of God; that ye may know that ye have eternal life, and that ye may believe on the name of the Son of God." Bible hope is a confident expectation in the promise of God.

I firmly believe that God has given us answers as to what happens to the most innocent of human life at death. The whereabouts of the innocent at death need not be a great mystery or just positive guesswork. God gave us the means to know exactly why and how these innocents gain entry into heaven.

In order to follow the course of this book, there are some things that must be considered by the reader. First, I am writing with the faith that the Bible is the word of God and it is correct in all matters that it addresses. There is no debate on the authority of Scripture in this book. Second, if the first point is correct, then all other writings outside of Scripture are subject to Scripture. No writing, tradition, church, religion, or scholar will outweigh the authority of Scripture. That seems easy and sensible enough to many; however, it is often negated once they realize that some of their own beliefs are only backed up by tradition and antiquity. Third, as with any Bible study, be prepared to change your belief to match Scripture. Some of the loudest voices I have heard, which cry out their militant stance against rank liberalism in Christianity, will also cower at the thought of going against the accepted teachings they learned in school or heard by one of their celebrity preachers.

My prayer is that this book can give you biblical answers to what happens to the innocents when they die. If you have suffered such a tragedy in your own family or friends, I hope you find comfort and knowledge in the pages of this book which endeavors to point you to the answers in the words of God.

God bless,
Robert Steven Hays, Sr.

Introduction

IT IS EASY TO make a generalized statement and say that in the case of a baby's death, they go to heaven. However, when it actually happens to someone you are involved with, it becomes a different matter. The parents or other loved ones want to know "for sure." That is when we must be able to give an answer that is definite in its foundation and confident in its assurance. By personal experience, I have found that I do not need to give a lengthy Bible study to parents when their child has died, but I do have to be able to look them in the eye and tell them that their baby is with Jesus, and do so with all honesty and assurance, having no doubt in my own heart. Often the case has been that as time passes, they will then ask questions that need biblical and detailed answers. The purpose of this book is to provide the scriptural confidence in the time of need and the detailed systematic answer when asked at a later date.

In writing a biblical answer, it is a necessity to trace the thread of that answer throughout Scripture. If the doctrine is to stand under the weight of scrutiny, it will also have to show its effect upon other major doctrines of Scripture. For this reason, it is essential that other doctrines must be examined for the cause and effect of this book's chosen topic. While trying to stay on point of the Main question, one must investigate other doctrines such as impeccability, predestination, extra-canonical writings, the Trinity, and the incarnation. The acceptance or rejection of each of these doctrines will also bear an enormous impact upon the doctrine of original sin and its effect on children.

This book lays out a scripturally based doctrine to answer the questions concerning the guilt of babies, their assurance of salvation, and the tenets by which a minister may comfort those who have suffered the loss of an innocent.

1

The Unanswered Questions

For those of us who believe the Bible to be true, there is a major problem which is not often addressed. We believe all are guilty of sin, as the Bible states in Rom 3:23, but when a baby dies, we also believe he or she goes to heaven. So, the question is "how?" Jesus is the only way to heaven according to John 14:6, but how does a child who cannot make the decision of receiving Christ get forgiveness of sin? Nobody wants to say that God would put an innocent baby in hell and nobody should! There is a scriptural answer that gives us a definite reason to believe that these innocents are safely and lovingly with the Lord at their death.

"The innocent" will be the term of choice throughout this writing used to describe babies and young children, those born with mental disabilities, and those who acquired a mental disability at a young age. This entire group of persons should also be considered when the reference is to children, babies, or infants, whether in my writing or that of a quoted text.

Several years ago, in an ordination service for a junior minister, the ordination board proposed the question "What happens to infants at death?" After the candidate for the ordination declared ignorance of the topic, the elder ministers continued in a discussion among themselves. The discourse concluded with an inconclusive statement that although a minister should tell the parents of the deceased child that their baby is in heaven, the minister can possess no perfect confidence of the answer he is to give because of the acceptance of the doctrine of original sin. For one to accept that universally acclaimed doctrine, one must also realize there is no scriptural basis for allowing an infant into heaven, even though few would dare admit that a baby would be in hell. It was extremely disheartening to me to hear the misleading response. A minister of God stands in the place of Christ as stated in Scripture (2 Cor 5:20). That same minister must be able to comfort the bereaved with the confidence King David had when his own child died (2 Sam 12:23).

The purpose of this writing is to provide knowledge and confidence to those who grieve or minister that the Scripture gives a clear understanding that souls of infants shall be in heaven. A minister should be able to give answers to those who have lost their innocent loved ones.

It is understandable that those in the midst of their grief cannot be expected to wade through the theology and history needed to answer the question of salvation of the innocent. This book is written with the aim of providing the minister with confidence in his comfort to them as well as giving those parents the definitive answers they may need as time passes.

These answers need to be composed in an inclusive reasoning that draws upon the historical theology that has served the body of Christ while examining some of the historical errors as well. One cannot confuse truth with antiquity, as age cannot be the determining factor of doctrinal correctness or fallacy.

This book will seek to answer the dilemma of Adam's original sin in his descendants while yet some of those children of Adam are judged innocent at their death. An explanation of the doctrine of hamartiology (sin) must be given with its effects upon the human spirit, original sin, and the declaration of guilt or innocence.

Warning: as with the study of any biblical doctrine, there needs to be a willingness to change any belief if the tenets of a doctrine prove one's own thoughts to be erroneous. The Scriptures will always be the ultimate authority. This book does not debate the authoritativeness of Scriptures but will focus on answering the questions proposed with Scripture as the foundational authority.

THE MAIN QUESTION

The main question is, How do we know these innocents go to heaven? To answer this, we will seek to find what knowledge and actions an individual of limited mental capacity or capability may have but are still judged innocent by God.

Hell, and subsequently the lake of fire, is an eternal terrible place. The thought of such is somewhat incomprehensible to man's mind, and yet it is the place of sin and those who refused to repent. With such a horrible destiny in mind, it would be cruel to not give a clear-cut, definitive boundary of what would demand someone deserving such an eternity.

An illustration of this would be the threat of severe punishment if one were to cross a certain boundary. The problem would be if that boundary was not a clearly defined line in the sand. This would produce a person who is constantly in fear of crossing a line of which they have no actual knowledge. The result would be neurosis or psychosis, which eventually could become apathy and rebellion.

The purpose of this main question is to define that line in the sand which would cause someone to be held guilty in the eyes of God and to be deserving of eternal damnation. Do young children who die go to hell?

Throughout biblical history there seems to be a lack of addressing the questions of when, how, and why a person is declared guilty in the eyes of God in a simple yet formulaic way. This would comprise tracing the subject of infant death, guilt, or innocence throughout Scripture rather than simply finding a verse to back up a preconceived ideology. The answers that are usually given lack a definitive quality to those who would quote seemingly opposed Scriptures. Basing answers on a singular idea or emotion without regard to the biblical questions that arise from these answers is unacceptable. The answer must stand the scrutiny of a Genesis to Revelation study.

The Augustinian definition of original sin supposes that a child is born with the guilt of Adam's sin. There seems to be a consensus amongst Romans and Protestants alike to align themselves with the commonly accepted teaching of original sin as Augustine expounds it. The main problem with these teachings still roams about unanswered: What is the line that must be crossed to declare a soul sinful in the eyes of God? Do babies go to hell? Their heartless affirmation may have been acceptable in the medieval ages of superstition, ignorance, and serfdom, but an answer of putting children in hell will not be acceptable to most societies or denominations in this age.

Theology must stand upon the words of God regardless of the society in which it ministers. However, to do so, theology must have solid answers upon which to make that stand. Traditions and catechisms which are based upon teachings that are accepted only because of their antiquity, as well as popular social opinions, only confuse the answers when there is no scriptural foundation upon which they are built.

THE BASIC QUESTIONS THAT NEED TO BE ANSWERED

The First Basic Question

In order to answer the main question, one must separate it into several basic questions. The first of these basic questions would be, What is the difference between disobedience and unrighteousness?

As Adam is the first of humanity and establishes the pattern that we follow, it is necessary to discern what Adam would have known before his fall into sin. Young children of the present generation possess this same knowledge, but are they held accountable for sin? To answer this first basic question shows the difference between disobedience to a stated command and what violates the laws of righteousness. This difference will define the boundary that would make a person guilty of damnation in the judgment of God, which is the groundwork of answering the main question.

Genesis 2:16–17 (KJV) records the command of God to Adam concerning the tree of knowledge of good and evil. "And the LORD God commanded the man, saying, Of every tree of the garden thou mayest freely eat: But of the tree of the knowledge of good and evil, thou shalt not eat of it: for in the day that thou eatest thereof thou shalt surely die."

Considering these two verses and the command that is given, one must note that Adam understood some things which are not usually attributed to his pre-sinful state. Adam knew what good was. God is good, and Adam walked with God daily. Adam knew the concept of disobedience as he was instructed what not to do. Adam also would have realized what judgment for disobedience was because God warned him of a pending death for any disobedience.

Adam must have known of the process of death in some capacity, howbeit in a limited fashion. A tree that brings forth fruit would also have buds and blooms that eventually die out to make way for the fruit. This would be the reason Adam was told to dress the garden and keep it (Gen 2:15). This circle of physical life would have resulted from the cycles God set in order when designing the creation and could be seen in the plants and animals. There is no scriptural evidence to say that the animals did not go through the natural cycles of life and death before the fall. Humanity would have been exempt from the pattern of life and death as God created Adam in his own image. That would explain why man's death sentence applied only upon the choice of Adam to commit the sin of disobedience.

For the Lord God to say that Adam had become "as one of us, to know good and evil" must have a broader connotation than is usually applied. The relationship of good and evil, along with righteousness and sin, must be delved into in order to explain Adam's pre-fall knowledge and exactly what knowledge was imparted to Adam upon eating of that forbidden tree.

A young child would have knowledge of obedience and disobedience. This writing will show the reason why a disobedient child may still be viewed as innocent in the judgment of sin.

There is much written of the tree of the knowledge of good and evil; however, there is less written on the delineation between righteousness and goodness. There is a definitive line between what can be defined as good and what can be defined as righteous.

One can see the biblical aspect of this conundrum in Exod 32:14: "And the LORD repented of the evil which he thought to do unto his people." God is good according to the Scripture (Ps 52:1) and the devils are evil (Acts 19:15–16). The simple ideology is that God is always good, and the devils are always evil. That concept will not withstand scrutiny. Goodness can become a sinful situation as Satan appears as an angel of light (2 Cor 11:14). Evil can also be the righteous response from God (Exod 32:14). There needs to be set forth a biblical definition to each of these words in order to approach the problem within defined parameters.

Goodness without righteousness can become, cause, or invoke evil in a multitude of ways. Eve saw the tree was good for food (Gen 3:6), and yet it produced evil in the world. The religious will do many good works and yet their judgment will declare them to be evil (Matt 7:21–23). One cannot have a biblical discussion of good and evil without including the topic of righteousness.

The Second Basic Question

The second basic question that follows is, How did Adam's sin affect all of mankind?

The Scripture states that for some of Adam's descendants, God does not impute unto them sin (Rom 5:13). Therefore, there must be a definitive line that would cause this action to take place. Scripture also states that Adam brought forth a son "in his own likeness, after his image" (Gen 5:3). The purpose of this question is to show the effect of Adam's sin upon all his descendants and to explain how their sins are not imputed at certain times. This question and explanation are necessary to further define the mechanics of

God's determination of guilt in each individual. If some are unaccountable for sin, then this sub-question is a requirement to see the biblical system whereby one may answer the main question: how do we know these innocents go to heaven, and what is the line in the sand that makes a person guilty in the judgment of God? Why does a dead infant not go to hell?

The concept of original sin and how it affects humanity has been a dilemma since man began putting his theology in print. The term "original sin" is often attributed to the teachings of Augustine. However, there are several other early church patriarchs that mention the subject but rather briefly. Augustine believed that the act of human copulation is in sinful concupiscence, and therefore, conception is a sin and continues the guilt of its parents. Philip Schaff notes that Augustine's idea of how a child inherits Adam's sin changes from time to time, which would show Augustine's uncertainty on the mode of transmission of the sin.[1]

The Third Basic Question

This third basic question is, Does Adam's sin automatically condemn every human to a judgment of hell?

The necessity of this question is one of comfort. It is not enough to tell grieving parents or loved ones that the minister "thinks" their child is in heaven. Those who have more than a shallow grasp of Christianity will require a biblical assurance of the destiny of their loved one. Following the first two basic questions, this third question and explanation will solidify the scriptural answer to the main question, How do we know these innocents go to heaven? Answering this question will provide comfort to the family who grieves, and to the minister by giving confidence to his answer. The purpose of pursuing this sub-question is to show that the innocent will not be in danger of eternal damnation.

Most modern theologians will agree that original sin condemns mankind in God's righteous judgment while making

---

1. Schaff, *On Marriage and Concupiscence.*

allowance for not putting babies in hell. There must be a doctrinal structure whereby the effects of original sin are reconciled with the declaration of innocence in children.

Included in the intention of this writing is the desire to give active ministers a substantive position on ministering to those suffering from the loss of their innocent loved ones. To try to alleviate the sufferings of the bereaved with platitudes that they do not fully believe themselves is hypocritical and self-serving.

OUR FOUNDATIONS:

The foundations will begin with the final authority. Scripture is the ultimate authority in all matters upon which the Bible speaks. God declares that his word is to be magnified above even his own name, as in Ps 138:2: "I will worship toward thy holy temple, and praise thy name for thy lovingkindness and for thy truth: for thou hast magnified thy word above all thy name." The Lord also declared that his words would be preserved as stated in Ps 12:6–7: "The words of the LORD [are] pure words: [as] silver tried in a furnace of earth, purified seven times. Thou shalt keep them, O LORD, thou shalt preserve them from this generation forever."

Although one must consider the historical positions of the church fathers and earlier theologians, antiquity cannot be the measure of final authority. As seen in the realm of the Roman church regarding the proclamation that there is now no limbo, the ancient authorities can change. The Protestant Martin Luther wrote anti-Semitic literature in his later years, which Adolf Hitler used in his own propaganda.[2]

Martin Luther's 1543 treatise titled "The Jews and Their Lies" is a compilation of vitriolic spewing in which the author condemns the Jewish people for being worse than heathens, liars and bloodhounds, possessed of the devil, and under the wrath of God. According to Luther, it is useless to try to reach them with

---

2. Olsen, *Luther and Hitler.*

the gospel.[3] Martin Luther accomplished many good works and is held in high esteem by many Protestants even to this day. His legacy includes the gospel left by his German translation of the Bible, his influence in German politics, and the founding of the German Reformation. Even so, five hundred years of time do not make this treatise on the Jews any more righteous than when it was first wickedly penned.

The second foundation is about the present state of mankind in sin. Scripture states that all have sinned (Rom 3:23). In this consideration it must be accounted that all who have the mental capacity to commit sin will eventually do so. The judgment is for everyone who could make a choice to sin regardless of whether or not they actually heard the gospel (Rev 20:11–15). This judgment will be based upon what they knew of righteousness and their conscience (Rom 2:14–15). Natural law, the knowledge of a person's conscience, will be a major factor in this judgment of mankind. This matter of innate knowledge and subsequent guilt will also be determinate factors in the judgment of the innocents.

Following the second foundation, Scripture also states that where there is no law there is no imputation of sin (Rom 5:13). This statement of innocence would therefore include babies and other innocents. Based upon this third foundation, there are some logical conclusions that are also backed up by various typologies of Scripture.

First, God would not put a baby in hell. God cursed those who burnt their children in the fires to Molech (Jer 32:35). God states emphatically in this passage that the idea to do so had not come into his mind. Second, no one suffers the eternal torment of the lake of fire for the sins of another. Revelation 20:12 records that each person is judged according to their own works, not those of another. Deuteronomy 24:16 also states that a child shall not be put to death for the sins of their father, which assumes the same law for the second death (Rev 21:8). Third, it is assumed the consensus of Augustine's original sin must be wrong. Adam's descendants inherit Adam's sin as stated in Rom 5:12. However, the

---

3. Luther, *Jews and Their Lies*.

death mentioned is the death of the body and not the spirit. Each person is therefore born with a living spirit (Rom 7:9). That living spirit then dies within everyone making a choice to sin (Eph 2:1).

It must, therefore, stand to reason that with these foundations there is also a definitive line of sin that is crossed for one to be condemned by the righteous judgment of God. God's laws and judgments are not ambiguous, nor are they arbitrary. The books are kept recording the actions of each individual, and those works are the condemnation of the soul. Therefore, it is assumed that the knowledge of righteousness, good, and evil is more complicated than many have considered. Thus, Adam had some knowledge of these subjects before the fall into sin.

SOME THINGS TO CONSIDER:

The first hypothesis is that Augustine's concept of original sin is based upon his own personal experience rather than on Scripture. The Roman church was still trying to find its doctrinal footing at the time of Augustine and therefore was susceptible to any theologies that seemed to have a systematic theme. The Protestant reformers kept Augustine's teaching in their movements. After these centuries of acceptance, many are unwilling to consider that this major tenet of so many Christian denominations could be in error.

Second, there is an explanation for why young children are not held accountable for sin. There is no scenario wherein God merely ignores sin and its judgment, nor does he sweep it under the carpet. All sin must be judged, and payment must be made. Therefore, there must be a doctrinal trail of the mechanics of their innocence.

Third, the knowledge of good and evil is reflected in the conscience of every man. With some, the realization of that knowledge is thwarted by a premature death or birth defect. That knowledge is more than a toddler knowing obedience or disobedience. God has a definitive line that once crossed, will kill the spirit of a man in trespasses and sins. This knowledge of good must also be reconciled with the knowledge of righteousness. The definition of these words has become cryptic through the years to the point of losing the doctrines that accompany the usage of such phrases.

2

How We Arrived Here

THIS CHAPTER WILL OUTLINE the various denominations and their historical teaching on infant sin and salvation. The purpose of this section is to show the steps many have followed while still failing to provide answers for those who grieve. If you are not interested in historical accounting, skip this chapter and turn to chapter three.

The famous debate between Augustine and Pelagius concerning original sin and its effect on Adam's descendants has never been fully resolved. It continues to be a contentious subject, as are Calvinism, eternal security, and dispensations. There are many unanswered questions concerning the mechanics of the "if" and "how" Adam's sin is passed down to all of Adam's children.

Original sin, as described by Augustine, is the guilt placed upon all people for the sin of Adam. The debate centers on the points of the reality of the person of Adam, the actuality of Adam's actions, and the extent of the effect of those actions by the first humans. There can be no shallow response to these questions by a serious student. The importance of this discourse on original sin is viewed in death's reality of the innocents. If all mankind is guilty of Adam's sin, then there must be provision for these who die without reaching a mental capacity of being able to understand the gospel. Would God, who is not willing that any should perish, then judge an infant guilty and banish them to the lake of fire for eternity? If one would say no to this question, then what would the system be for God not doing so?

Alan H. Hamilton writes an illustration of this puzzle. In his essay "The Doctrine of Infant Salvation," Hamilton writes concerning infant salvation within the Anglican Church and quotes the author W. H. Griffith Thomas. "But it may be pointed out that this view (Calvinism) does not really solve the problem, and the best foundation for believing in the salvation of all infants is pretty certainly to be seen in the universality of the Atonement of Christ. No question of election should be allowed to enter. Infants come into this world with the results of Adam's sin in them, and they are involved in the inherent sin of the race through the headship of our first parents. Whatever may be the meaning of St. Paul's word, "By the offense of one judgment was upon all men to condemnation," infants are assuredly included, but, on the other hand, they go out of this world equally associated with the world of the last Adam, the Lord from heaven. So that we can say of infants, "By the righteousness of One the free gift came upon all men to justification by Him."[1]

Although Thomas is very adamant in his belief of infant salvation, the statement gives no synopsis of how this infant salvation is to come into effect. If the idea of an infant experiencing the damnation of God in a lake of fire is abhorrent, there must be a biblical answer of more substance than one such as this which seems to be based upon emotion.

This chapter is to examine the concept of original sin through the ages, as well as how this doctrine affects infant salvation. This will include writing of the information of the Hebrew scholars of the Old Testament texts and attempt to trace the adaptation of the doctrine by the early church fathers. Did the Reformation theologians also carry this doctrine of original sin into their movements and denomination, and if so, how did they resolve the question of infant redemption? This writing will describe the evolution of the doctrine of original sin as well as the changes in the positions of infant salvation from differing sources.

---

1. Hamilton, "Doctrine of Infant Salvation," 472.

To lay the groundwork of the writing, one must begin with the definitions used in describing the tree that stands at the center of the debate: the tree of knowledge of good and evil. There seems to be much confusion on the question of what exactly is good and evil, compounded by not recognizing the contrast between good and righteous.

GOOD, EVIL, RIGHTEOUSNESS, AND THE TREE OF KNOWLEDGE

C. John Collins wrote an article for the *Southern Baptist Journal of Theology* in which he states,

> I hold that this tree is a means by which the humans were intended to acquire a knowledge of good and evil—if they stood the test, they would know good and evil from above, as those who have mastered temptation; sadly, they came to know good and evil from below, as those who have been mastered by temptation.[2]

Collins holds that Adam and Eve were innocent, but they were not "perfect." "Their task was to mature through the exercise of the obedience, to become confirmed in moral goodness."[3]

It is noted that God possesses the knowledge of good and evil, and yet it does not affect his righteousness. In this vein of thought, Collins suggests Adam was also meant to eventually possess this knowledge without it causing sin or detriment to holiness.

In writing for the *Westminster Biblical Journal*, William N. Wilder follows the same line of thought by saying "As such, the tree is a tree of wisdom."[4] The tree is a means of maturing wisdom regarding knowing what is good and evil. Wilder cites several scriptural examples of having the wisdom of good and evil, "like the angel of God." They describe King David with such an attribute in 2 Sam 14:17 and 2 Sam 14:20.

2. Collins, "Adam and Eve in the Old Testament," 13.
3. Collins, "Adam and Eve in the Old Testament," 13.
4. Wilder, "Illumination and Investiture," 54.

According to Collins and Wilder, the possession of the knowledge of good and evil is not an unrighteous thing of itself. How the knowledge came into possession is the real matter and the cause of the sin. Adam and Eve were trying to take a shortcut to spiritual maturity. This would be the same ideology that is stated in a response given by R. David Ibn Abi Zimra (1479–1573). This rabbi is known by the shortened Radbaz in the Responsa. Radbaz gives credit to Adam for a purity of heart in regard to his disobedience to God. Adam supposedly wanted to obtain eternal life for the sole purpose of being able to praise God for all of eternity. Adam's eating of the tree of life would have been encouraged because he saw that Eve now possessed knowledge she did not have previously. Adam surmised that if he ate of the tree, he would then possess the knowledge to know how to praise God correctly for all eternity.[5]

It is with interest to note the thoughts that the purpose of the tree in the garden is not just to serve as a tempting choice for Adam but that eventually God would have Adam eat of the tree with no ill outcome. God was waiting for Adam to "grow up" spiritually in order to be able to cope with the knowledge bestowed upon him. *The IVP Bible Background Commentary* states that with many of the religions of the world, the idea of "being like God" is the allure of immortality. This commentary states that this temptation to be like God was not immortality but rather obtaining the wisdom like God.[6]

Austin Freeman wrote his thesis titled "The Two Adams" with a comparison of Adam and Jesus Christ. In this essay, Freeman writes,

> But Adam was not merely a historical individual. He was the representative of all human beings, in whom humanity dwelled in a sort of dormancy. Adam had the unique position of being both the universal and the particular of humanity. He held within himself the potentiality of every human. His very name is simply the Hebrew word

---

5. Jacobs, *Theology in the Responsa*, 112.

6. Walton, et al., *IVP Bible Backgrounds Commentary*, 32

for "humanity," and is translated as such elsewhere in the Old Testament. Adam is not merely a man, but an archetype, a model not only of the second Adam but of humankind in general.[7]

Freeman's statement mentions that Adam is the archetype of all of humanity. With this concept in mind, Adam serves as a typology of the human experience on the path of sin, although it should be noted this is not the thesis of Freeman's paper.

The concept presented by Collins and Wilder contrasts with that of the Reformed theologians. David and Jonathan Gibson summarize the thoughts of these theologians by stating that "God entered into a covenant with Adam [as representative of his posterity] whereby he would reward Adam's obedience by giving him eternal life and punish his disobedience by death."[8]

The purpose of the tree in this theology is simply to test Adam's resolve. In the attempt to answer this question of why the tree was in the Garden, Gibson writes,

> One should not go beyond these attempted explanations: due to debilitating deficiencies of his understanding and perversions of his will, man has sinned; and God allowed it. Scripture does not allow us to probe this mystery beyond the realization of its reality; proper human humility should incline us to realize that our finite minds will not be able to comprehend this mystery.[9]

It would seem their response is to leave these things to the unexplained and to accuse one of having a presumptuous spirit in seeking a more definitive answer.

John Goldingay combines the thoughts of Gibson with that of Wilder and Collins. In his Old Testament Theology series, Goldingay writes,

> Adam and Eve did not gain knowledge of everything as a result of eating the tree's fruit . . . but discernment

7. Freeman, *Two Adams*, 2–3.
8. Gibson and Gibson, *From Heaven He Came and Sought Her*, 216.
9. Gibson and Gibson, *From Heaven He Came and Sought Her*, 176.

between good and bad enables someone to make proper decisions. It is thus a mark of maturity and insight . . . and it is natural enough that God should have provided a way of gaining this knowledge, but very surprised that God should have prohibited access to it.[10]

Goldingay continues this discourse by giving a comparison to Genesis chapter 22 and explains that as God tested Abraham, he first tested Adam. Adam had to be willing to submit to the time and place of God's choosing to receive that knowledge. He, of course, failed in this test of patience.

Although Matthew Henry is not considered an academic by some, his quote is included in the work of William G. T. Shedd, which gives it credence to be quoted in this writing. In their comments of Henry, he expresses his opinion that the tree gave no actual knowledge, nor did it have any intrinsic properties to bestow upon the first couple.

> The tree of the knowledge of good and evil was so called not because it had any virtue in it to further or increase useful knowledge, for surely then it would not have been forbidden: but (1) because there was an express positive revelation of the will of God concerning this tree . . . what is good? Tis good not to eat of this tree. What is evil? Tis evil to eat of this tree. The distinction between all other moral good and evil was written in the heart of a man by nature, but this which results from a positive law was written upon this tree.[11]

The quotation by Henry and recorded by Shedd would seem to indicate they thought the tree only imparted a sense of guilt of disobedience. This emotion would be the experience of a child, who is innocent, but upon disobeying a parent, that child finds himself with an awful sense of guilt.

Much is made of the tree's imparting of knowledge concerning good and evil; however, in regard to infant guilt and salvation,

10. Goldingay, *Israel's Gospel*, 132.
11. Shedd, *Dogmatic Theology*, 547.

one must consider the difference between good and righteousness as well as the biblical definitions of good, evil, and righteousness.

The paper written by Klaus Detlev Shulz is on the topic of the two types of righteousness, as presented by Luther and Melanchthon.[12] Shulz presents the teachings of these men, as well as others, and the acceptance of their teachings in the Book of Concord. The Book of Concord defines these two types of righteousness:

> This article makes the important distinction between the two kinds of righteousness. The first righteousness comes through the Holy Spirit and the word. It is called passive righteousness, spiritual righteousness, or the righteousness of God *(Justicia Dei)*. It is associated with internal movements, such as the fear of God, trust in God, and patience, which natural man cannot produce on his own. The other righteousness is that which humans create actively in the civil realm among one another by use of their free will and reason and through the outward performance of "good deeds."[13]

These two types of righteousness play a major role in the theology of those who would delve into the knowledge of children and their salvation. Often, civil righteousness is confused with the knowledge of how to be part of the salvation plan. Likewise, to violate that righteousness is seen as violating the standard of God and thus condemns one to damnation.

Scripture states that every man is given the natural laws of God written upon his heart (Rom 2:14–15). This natural law must be more than a civil righteousness if it is going to condemn one to the lake of fire for eternity. A toddler would know somewhat of the civil law that governs its family and home, but does that toddler understand the natural law of the righteousness of God? Melanchthon describes natural law as "a natural law is a common judgment to which all men alike assent, and therefore one which God has inscribed upon the soul of each man, adopted to form and

---

12. Shulz, *Two Kinds of Righteousness*, 17–40.

13. Shulz, *Two Kinds of Righteousness*, 19.

shape character."[14] This natural law is the knowledge of the first type of righteousness, that of God.

Melanchthon outlines his ideas of civil law, which comprise good works.[15] For one to assume that civil righteousness grants justification before God would be a grave mistake. Melanchthon praised certain philosophers and stated the need for humanity to be part of society. He also states that philosophy fails in its answers because of its rejection of the concept of original sin.[16] This accusation of failure to answer will boomerang back to Melanchthon because babies would not be capable of possessing either type of the knowledge of righteousness that he and Luther describe.

Further complications arise when one considers the lack of uniform definitions while using the same phraseology. Paul R. Harris, a Lutheran pastor, wrote a treatise on the opposition between civil righteousness and civil religion. Harris gives an entirely different definition of civil righteousness than Luther and Melanchthon:

> There is a distinction between civil righteousness and civil religion. To endorse the one is to not endorse the other. Civil righteousness is a gift of God to fallen mankind through the law. Civil religion, on the other hand, is a creation of men and interferes with the gospel. It can never be in accord with God's will.[17]

Harris equates civil righteousness with the law but also with the gospel. This would be of great concern in the attempt to explain infant salvation. Melanchthon's explanation has a more biblical ring to it regarding trying to understand what the line in the sand is that would justify God's condemnation of the soul. To "break the rules" is not an adequate line in the sand when one must consider the mental capability of the person involved.

---

14. Melanchthon, *Loci Communes*, 112.
15. Melanchthon, *Loci Communes*, 11.
16. Gerrish, *Grace and Reason*, 3.
17. Harris, *Civil Righteousness versus Civil Religion*, 25.

The Christian should not view the morals of good and evil without considering the righteousness of God. As an example, Scott R. Paeth penned an article on the moral dilemma of video games.[18] This is a contemporary article that does not consider original sin or the stain of that sin upon children, although it is written in the context of the effect of video games on children from a Christian perspective. The conflict in this article is seen in the equating of good with righteousness. It does not mention righteousness in the article. This brings up the modern enigma of making something good, the equivalent of making it righteous. Eve saw the tree was good in ways, but that by no means justified it to be righteous as a source of food. The contemporary societal modus operandi seems to be to find the good in something, and therefore, it becomes right.

If one were to examine evil in the Scripture, the usual definitions would be adequate in most uses of the word. An examination of Exod 32:14 will cause consternation in the theology of some: "And the LORD repented of the evil which he thought to do unto his people." Unless one is to accuse the Scripture of being wrong, it must be accepted that God was going to cause evil to Israel. Suffice it to say that evil is not always unrighteous. An article in the *Heythrop Journal* states that the compatibility of belief in an omnibenevolent, omnipotent God and the reality of suffering, pain, death, and evil has long been a preoccupation of both theists and atheists, and the problem of evil, the problem of theodicy, is no closer to a definitive answer despite the best efforts of numerous scholars.[19]

The fact that Adam knew some of the details of evil before his fall would give occasion to state that a young child may also know and still be innocent. Adam knew the punishment for his transgression, as God had told him he would die if he ate the fruit. A child would know the punishment for the transgression of touching the fragile glass on a table after being told not to do so. Would that knowledge in itself be enough to condemn a soul?

18. Paeth, "Virtual Good and Evil," 22–25.
19. Otto, *Theism, Evil, and the Search for Answers*, 136–40.

THE HEBREW SCHOLARS

The foundation of the New Testament is the Old Testament. It is not possible to study the doctrines of the New Testament without a knowledge of the Hebrew texts. Hebrew writings and academia use several major sources. These are given certain weight according to the author or student who may hold one source to be of more value than another. The Torah, which is usually the Pentateuch, is described as the revelation that is given by divine inspiration from God. The Kabbalah is the mystical interpretation of the Bible. The Talmud is the literary work of eight centuries of scholars regarding study and discussion of the Torah. The Responsa is answers to questions on Jewish law by scholars. This list is not exhaustive, but with these various sources of authority, the answers found may be confusing and contradictory.

Samuel S. Cohon of the Hebrew Union College in Cincinnati states that the narrative of Genesis chapter 3 is "one of the most influential biblical chapters in human thought."[20] Mr. Cohon continues with his opinion by writing that although regarded as a doctrine of original sin by Pauline Christians, this chapter does not teach a doctrine of the fall of humanity entirely, nor does it expound on a sin passed down by genetic reproduction.

One of Mr. Cohon's arguments consists of the importance the other biblical authors place upon the narration of the paradise story. When asked the question of what was made of this story by the rest of the Bible, he answered "hardly any."[21] Cohon's interpretation of Ps 51:7 is that it records the general inclination of mankind toward sin, rather than making the act of procreation to be sin. This concept of placing original sin transmission in the act of coitus will play a significant part in the biblical ideology of the church fathers.

Mr. Cohon lists three views held by rabbinical scholars on the fall of mankind.[22] First, some consider this act of Adam to have a

---

20. Cohon, "Original Sin," 276.
21. Cohon, "Original Sin," 282.
22. Cohon, "Original Sin," 296.

corrupting effect on all of Adam's race. The second view is rather vague. It states there is a connection of Adam's sin to mankind's general guilt but does so without any actual explanation. The third view is the one most held by rabbinic Judaism. This teaching is that each person is responsible for their own conduct, and it is not influenced by the sin of Adam. Mr. Cohon does write that "Rabbinic views on the subject have the character of random, informal, and private opinions without dogmatic import whatsoever."[23]

The Encyclopedia of the Jewish Religion gives a somewhat contradictory answer to the question of Christian belief in original sin. In these writings of Jewish scholars, much is made by the comparison of supposed Christian theology in order to vindicate Jewish theology. This volume states that Christian ideology of original sin is that Adam's sin involved all of mankind so that only a divine act can save them. It further states that rabbis did not teach general sin but do often hold the doctrinal view that all men die because of Adam's transgression.[24]

The compiled work of editor Louis Jacobs consists of opinions given over a span of one thousand years by Jewish scholars, teachers, and rabbis. These are answers (Responsa) to questions of the Jewish law and its effects upon the Jewish people.

Jacobs records the thought of Ibn David. When asked about original sin, Ibn David answered with a reference to the Talmud which he interprets as saying that Eve had sexual intercourse with the serpent in the garden, and thus, all of her descendants were made sinful. Ibn David further states that upon approaching Sinai, Israel is thus freed from the taint of "original sin."[25] Ibn David's response would seem to place the burden of original sin upon Eve rather than Adam.

Joel Rembaum writes of medieval Jewish thought in regard to the doctrine of original sin. He quotes an anonymous sixteenth-century writer as penning the idea that if one could disprove the Christian concept of original sin, the whole of Christendom would

23. Cohon, "Original Sin," 296–97.

24. Werblowsky and Wigoder, *Encyclopedia of the Jewish Religion*, 141.

25. Jacobs, *Theology in the Responsa*, 50.

fall apart at the foundation.[26] Rembaum records the thoughts of Yair ben Shabbetai of Correggio in regard to the teaching of Gen 2:17. This teacher, along with several of his contemporaries, acknowledges that Adam's sin resulted in the physical death of humanity, but in no way does it infer the spiritual death of all. The suggestion that Adam's sin would cause the eternal punishment of his descendants would, in their view, violate the Scriptures recorded in Deut 24:16 and Ezek 18:20: Fathers shall not be put to death for their children, nor children for the fathers: a man shall be put to death only for his own sin. Rembaum states that considering these clear verses of Scripture, the idea of damnation by original sin would appear to the Jewish scholars of the day as not only a contradiction in God's justice but also a blasphemy against the righteousness of God.[27]

Cohon carries this same thought into modern Hebrew theology. Eve's culpability is addressed in the modern writing of Samuel Cohon when he states that "even the more mystic among them who admit that the pollution of the serpent infected humanity refuse to consider human nature as hopelessly corrupted."[28] In this same passage, Cohon states that every person has complete responsibility for their own acts and guilt of sin. The capacity to do good is the image of God impressed upon mankind.

The question of infant salvation is then addressed amidst the rather confusing statements of whether there is in fact an original sin that must be appeased. Making another supposed comparison to Christian writings whereby they assume all Christians regard the escape of damnation through the baptism of water, Rabbinic Judaism taught that circumcision is the means of salvation. Cohon gives the teachings of Rabbi Levi which taught that Abraham would forbid any from entering the gates of hell who were circumcised Jews.[29] The question is then asked, what about a circumcised Jew whose life is unworthy of redemption? The answer given by Levi

---

26. Rembaum, "Medieval Jewish Criticism," 357.

27. Rembaum, "Medieval Jewish Criticism," 358.

28. Cohon, "Original Sin," 330.

29. Cohon, "Original Sin," 323.

is that the foreskin of uncircumcised babies is taken from them and placed upon the unworthy circumcised Jew.[30] These answers provided by rabbis do not take into account the gentile infants that die, as well as the state of those uncircumcised babies who are waiting to be circumcised in the afterlife.

The Encyclopedia of the Jewish Religion places a major emphasis upon circumcision of baby boys.[31] Elijah is the patron saint of circumcision. An empty chair is present at the circumcision ceremony to acknowledge that Elijah's spirit is present at all Jewish circumcisions. There is to be no excuse for not circumcising the boy on his eighth day unless it is for medical reasons. Further, every Jewish boy shall be circumcised unless he has had two previous siblings die from the procedure. The circumcision is the most significant symbol of the covenant between God and Israel.

The consensus which would still be much debated among some Jewish scholars seems to be that there is no recognition of the doctrine of original sin; however, there remains the need of circumcision to take away the sin inherited from Adam. Confusion is added to the material because of foundations made by Jewish scholarship concerning Christian doctrines.

Medieval Jewish rabbis wrote some official replies to the question of original sin on the basis that Christianity teaches across the board the doctrine of total depravity. Total depravity is a concept often associated with the five points of Calvinism. Many would mistakenly state their agreement with this doctrine because of Rom 3:23 without considering what is actually being claimed by its proponents. Total depravity is the teaching that mankind's fall in Adam is so complete that he is unable to even choose to accept the grace of God. God must therefore regenerate a man, and then that man is able to choose Christ. The basis of this false doctrine contradicts the explicit teaching of Eph 1:13 which states, "In whom ye also *trusted*, after that ye heard the word of truth, the gospel of your salvation: in whom also after that ye believed, ye

---

30. Cohon, "Original Sin," 323.

31. Werblowsky and Wigoder, *Encyclopedia of the Jewish Religion*, 90.

were sealed with that holy Spirit of promise." Faith, belief, and trust are prerequisites to salvation and the sealing of the Holy Spirit.

The erroneous foundation that all Christians believe in the inability of man to do anything good or to choose anything good is one of the reasons given for Jewish rejections of Jesus.[32] Brown quotes Aryeh Kaplan's book *The Real Messiah*, showing Kaplan's objections to salvation in Christ by saying, "what sin was so great that it required his sacrifice? The early Christians answered that this was required to atone for the sin of Adam, as if all human culpability were Adam's and none was our own."[33]

The topic of sins of the parents is addressed by Dov Weiss in his paper regarding the rabbinic teaching. Weiss realizes the contradictory and unclear statements by many of the teaching rabbis as well as those adopted by the early church fathers. Weiss takes note that the gnostics, among others, were so belabored by the task of reconciling what to do with children and inherited sin that they finally concluded the "Old Testament God is either morally imperfect, or worse, outright evil."[34]

The rabbis eventually made some concessions of their own in order to make the Scripture fit their code of moral conduct. According to Weiss, midrashic texts by rabbis of the seventh century AD reinterpreted the texts of Exod 20 and Exod 34.[35] These rabbis conceded that although God did give the original principle of punishing the children for the sins of the parents, God then repents of his commands upon the intercession of Moses upon ethical grounds. Weiss gives a synopsis of this midrash by Menachem Fisch in which Fisch states,

> God is astonishingly described as having produced a morally deficient early draft of the Torah, [and then] Moses is portrayed as having refused to comply, and having challenged it on moral grounds . . . [the theology] is subsequently described as having been happily revised

32. Brown, *Answering Jewish Objections*, 198.
33. Brown, *Answering Jewish Objections*, 301n320.
34. Weiss, "Sins of the Parents," 1.
35. Weiss, "Sins of the Parents," 12.

by virtue of God accepting Moses's superior moral judgment.[36]

The conclusion of the Hebrew scholars seems to be to remain vague concerning any definitive statements on original sin and its effect upon Adam's descendants. This raises unanswered questions concerning the need of infant circumcision, Abraham's guarding of the gates of hell to prevent circumcised Jews from entering in, and the inclination of mankind to sin. Many of their answers stem from reflexive reactions to the theology presented by the Roman church. Until the time of Augustine and his followers, the Jewish scholars were content to leave the matter of original sin to a minor role in the theology of the Old Testament.

EARLY CHURCH FATHERS

When speaking of the early church fathers on the topic of original sin and infant salvation, one would eventually find Augustine to be the authoritative voice on the subject. Augustine's statement in his *The City of God* is based on his own interpretation of Rom 5:12.

> God, the Author of all natures, but not of the defects, created man good; but man, corrupt by the choice and condemned by justice, has produced a descendants that is both corrupt and condemned. For, we all existed in that one man, since, taken together, we were the one man who fell into sin through the woman who was made out of him before sin existed. Although the specific form by which each of us was to live was not yet created and assigned, our nature was already present in the seed from which we were to spring. And because this nature has been soiled by sin and doomed to death and justly condemned, no man was to be born of man in any other condition.[37]

36. Weiss, "Sins of the Parents," 13n41.

37. Augustine, *City of God*, 278–79.

Michael M. Christensen's paper "Original Sin from Justin Martyr to Augustine" is a very concise synopsis of the beliefs of early church fathers on the topic of original sin and its effect on infants.[38] Christensen reaches the conclusion that the early church scholars before Augustine did not give much consideration to this topic of Adam's sin, as they followed the lead of the Hebrew scholars. He begins his essay with Justin Martyr and documenting Justin's non-acceptance of a doctrine of original sin tainting humanity.[39]

Christensen continues his writing in the teachings of Theophilus of Antioch, Irenaeus, Clement of Alexandria, and Origen. The views of these men on the effect of Adam's fall may differ from each other, but none would agree with the statements of Augustine on this subject. Some, such as Irenaeus, would attribute human death to Adam but not the spiritual corruption of all humanity. Others, like Origen, regard the entire narrative of Adam and Eve's existence in a garden to be mythological and used as an allegory in order to give some moral lesson. The early church fathers that do take a literal view of Adam and Eve's existence generally agree that man's mortality is a result of Adam's sin while individual corruption is by individual choice.

Christensen records the thoughts of Theodore of Mopsuestia stating in Theodore's commentary on the book of Psalms that the idea of inherited spiritual corruption is foolish.[40] He further writes that "Children come into the world with no burden of sin."[41]

It is not until the teaching of Ambrose that the doctrine of infant corruption becomes a major teaching. However, Christensen again records Ambrose and his biblical contradictions by writing that Ambrose seems to change position on the guilt of mankind. Ambrose gives place to allowing that all of humanity is culpable in Adam's sin and guilt, while then stating at other times

---

38. Christensen, *Original Sin*, 1.

39. Justin Martyr, *Dialogue with Trypho*, 124, 341.

40. Christensen, *Original Sin*, 9.

41. Christensen, *Original Sin*, 9.

each human is guilty only of their own sins.[42] Infant salvation then must become a part of the conversation, and Ambrose teaches that baptism removes the guilt of our own sins and foot-washing removes the stain of Adam's sin. Augustine then picks up this mantle of Ambrose and becomes the authoritative voice of the Roman Church, and thus, many of the Protestant churches.

THE EARLY EASTERN CHURCH

Irenaeus of Lyons (Late 100s AD)

Irenaeus commented several times on the topic of original sin; howbeit, some of his comments were ambiguous and could be interpreted in opposing ways. Because of the lack of terminology, specifically "original sin," the syntax and rhetoric used can be construed by either side of the argument in order to support their theology. The pivotal word would be "death." Is he speaking of physical death of the body or spiritual death of the soul?

In the book titled *Against Heresies* by Irenaeus, he recounts the Genesis story. In doing so, Irenaeus stresses the punishment of Adam to be physical death. His picture of redemption is that Jesus Christ conquered that physical death for us.[43] Throughout the pages of his book, Irenaeus constantly refers to the punishment of God as being physical death which is passed along to humanity. The concept of spiritual death being an inherited trait would seem to be foreign to the theology of Irenaeus.[44]

Irenaeus does not debate the topic in detail due to the main issue of his writing being the refutation of the gnostic heresies. The gnostics denied the very incarnation of God in Christ as well as other basic teachings, so Irenaeus was more inclined to engage in those doctrines.

---

42. Christensen, *Original Sin*, 11.

43. Irenaeus. *Against Heresies.*

44. Irenaeus. *Against Heresies.*

Tertullian (200 AD)

Tertullian was to become the bishop of Africa, and thus, is considered one of the more authoritative church fathers in history. In his writings, Tertullian places the emphasis on the condemnation of man squarely on the shoulders of Satan rather than Adam. It is Satan's seed rather than Adam's that causes our condemnation.

> Finally, in every instance of vexation, contempt, and abhorrence, you pronounce the name of Satan . . . through whom Man was deceived in the very beginning so that he transgressed the command of God. On account of his transgression Man was given over to death, and the whole human race, which was infected by his seed, was made the transmitter of condemnation.[45]

Again, because of the lack of explanation by the original author, many theologians can interpret these writings to suggest a myriad of opinions. Gregg Allison demonstrates this point by giving the quote of Tertullian in which he states sin is the "evil which arises from its [the soul's] corrupt origin."[46] Allison inserts the words "the souls" to give credence to the doctrine of original sin corrupting the spirit of the infant. Tertullian does not make such a clear claim on the matter.

Cyprian (250 AD)

Cyprian became the Bishop of Carthage. His writings on the concept of sin passed down to the descendants of Adam are expressed in a treatise in which he uses the example of a baby who has died. In doing so, Cyprian seems to place emphasis on the flesh of the child bearing Adam's sinful nature rather than the spirit, which would still be pure. "How much rather ought we to shrink from hindering an infant, who, being lately born, has not sinned, except in that, being born after the flesh according to Adam, he has

---

45. Tertullian, *Testimony of the Soul*, 22.
46. Allison, *Historical Theology*, 344.

contracted the contagion of the Ancient Death . . . that to him are remitted, not his own sins, but the sins of another."[47]

In the quotation of Cyprian that is documented by Gregg Allison, Allison gives the idea that Cyprian believed in the corruption of the human soul from birth. "This recently born infant has not sinned except that, being born physically according to Adam, he has contracted the contagion [infection] of the ancient death at his birth. Thus, he more easily approaches the reception of the forgiveness of sins because the sins forgiven are not his own but those of another."[48]

This statement of Cyprian is one that can be used by differing sides of the argument. Is Cyprian stating that mankind is evil at birth in his soul or that sin is inherited in the flesh of a child? From this statement, either side of the debate could use the same reference.

As noted in the previous chapter, Origen regarded the Genesis account to be mythological rather than an actual account of an individual man named Adam.[49] This exegesis resulted in his dismissal as an authoritative voice on this matter. The other theologians mentioned who are contemporary of this time period make an accurate representation in displaying the lack of definition of original sin as was later ascribed to the writing of Augustine. To suggest that these early Christian patriarchs did not believe the spirit of an individual descendant of Adam was contaminated by Adam's sin is a very plausible supposition that cannot be disproved by the patriarchal writings.

THE WESTERN CHURCH

The Roman Church's influence became the authoritative voice for much of Western theology and philosophy. This is also the case in the doctrine of original sin. Although the concept of individuals

---

47. Cyprian, *Epistles of Cyprian*, 198.
48. Allison, *Historical Theology*, 344.
49. Origen, *Writings*, 206.

born bearing the guilt of Adam's sin is mentioned, the exact nature of that burden was not defined until Augustine set it into systematic theology. Most Western thought on the subject can be traced to his writings.

Augustine (400 AD)

Mircea Eliade gives credit to Augustine by writing, "he is justly considered to be the greatest and most influential of all Western theologians."[50] Augustine is credited with coining the phrase "original sin." It is his essays on the subject that gave credence to the postulation that the spirit is born with Adam's sin. In his book *Confessions*, Augustine writes: ". . . and I was going down to hell, carrying all the sins which I had committed both against thee and myself, and others, many and grievous, over and above the bond of original sin, whereby we all die in Adam."[51]

Augustine makes it clear that his concept of original sin will assign anyone to the pits of condemnation rather than just mortal death. Eliade notes that Augustine's struggle with his own sexual sins gave occasion to his shift in philosophy which began in the Manichaean community.[52] While the personal struggle of Augustine with his own concupiscence is well documented by several sources of Augustinian biography, it is also plainly read in the words of Augustine himself in his *Confessions*.[53] The battle of his personal sexual addiction was to have an extreme effect on his theology.

Ken Wilson summarizes the influences on Augustine's life, which, although it can explain some of Augustine's thoughts, can also add to the confusing positions within his theology. Dr. Wilson states:

---

50. Eliade, *History of Religious Ideas*, 42.
51. Augustine, *Book of Confessions*, 84.
52. Eliade, *History of Religious Ideas*, 42.
53. Augustine, *Confessions of St. Augustine*, 20.

Scholars have identified Stoicism, Neoplatonism, and Gnostic Manichaeism as important influences on Augustine of Hippo. He spent years personally involved in these three extremely deterministic philosophies. The terms fate and predestination carry considerable philosophical and Biblical connotations. Therefore, I coined the phrase Divine Unilateral Predetermination of Individuals' Eternal Destinies (DUPIED) to explore the similarities and differences between pagan and Christian literature without importing biased concepts.[54]

Wilson further describes each of these influences as well as some of their unscriptural doctrines. Augustine struggled with some of these pagan concepts for many years.

Augustine was not sure he even wanted to be delivered from his sexual sins at one point. This idea of having to abstain from sex became a temporary hindrance to Augustine becoming a Christian.[55] In coming to grips with his addiction, Augustine also hardened his belief in the source of his concupiscence coming from the sins of his parents' sexual act. His biblical text for this thought comes from a personal interpretation of Ps 51:5 which requires an entire chapter of his confessions to understand his point.[56] Jesse Couenhoven of Villanova University quotes an unfinished work from Augustine to Julian in which Augustine explicitly expresses that "Those born from the union of bodies are under the power of the devil before they are reborn . . . because they are born through that concupiscence by which the flesh has desires opposed to the spirit."[57]

To understand the extent of Augustine's dogma, one must consider the apologetics of his particular philosophy in his debate with the Pelagian adherents. Augustine wrote an epistle to answer Pelagius's attack upon the teachers of original sin as taught by himself. In the tract, Pelagius is quoted as asking the question "by

54. Wilson, *Foundation of Augustinian-Calvinism*, 5.

55. Sorabji, *Emotion and Peace of Mind*, 400.

56. Augustine, *St. Augustine's Confessions*, 23.

57. Couenhoven, *Augustine's Doctrine of Original Sin*, 385.

what means is sin discovered in an infant?"[58] Augustine answers that query in his philosophical style and by quoting Rom 5. His application of the Pauline epistle is that "death" is a spiritual death passed upon all men. Augustine further restates the question and then comments, "Let him now believe in original sin. Let him permit infants to come to Christ that they may be saved."[59]

Pelagius (400 AD)

Pelagius was a theologian of British ancestry. He was very much an advocate of free will as well as some other unpopular beliefs. Pelagius is the "villain" of the biblical world in regard to original sin. He was censured by the Pope and vilified by men such as Augustine.[60] Pelagius taught that man was not incapable of making the choice of good or evil. His thought of original sin was that it still left the man with the ability to choose to yield to temptation or not. This obviously flew in the face of those who taught definite atonement of the elect. Augustine and later Martin Luther are both credited with teaching that atonement was only for the elect, thereby denying the possibility that a man would actually "choose" to do right or be redeemed.[61]

Many of the theologians have made Pelagius a target of their disdain and the epitome of heresy. Pelagianism is a derisive term for those who reject the traditional stand of predestination, election, and original sin. It must be accounted that this book is not advocating many of the teachings of Pelagius but merely demonstrates there are alternate views of the effects of original sin. The modern concept of Pelagianism is that one can achieve salvation through the means of their own good works and choices.

Much of the surviving work of Pelagius seems to be fragmented copies. That seems rather odd, considering how much his

---

58. Augustine, *Anti-Pelagian Works*, 187.

59. Augustine, *Anti-Pelagian Works*, 187.

60. Phipps, *Heresiarch*, 124–33.

61. Lopes Pereira, *Augustine of Hippo and Martin Luther*, 505.

"heresies" are quoted by opposing theologians. In reconstructing the Pelagian works on the defense of free will, Daniel Jennings writes,

> Unfortunately for those wishing to fully understand Pelagius' views, archenemy Augustine is not a faithful quoter when it comes to his archenemy's writings. Augustine will quote him in one place, then repeat the quote later in a different way, each time wording it in such a way that best suits his argument.[62]

As is often the case with human nature, people tend to want to put their enemies in the worst light possible, and therefore the quotation of their sayings can be skewered. This is noted by Michael Axworthy in his treatise on the revenge of Pelagius. He describes the battle of the two theologians as Pelagius being the proponent of free will and Augustine being the voice of opposition with his teaching of original sin. Axworthy states,

> Augustine's interpretation of original sin, closely associated with sexuality, also facilitated the misogyny of the medieval church. But Pelagius has had the last laugh in the liberal, humanist culture of western Europe today. Generally, we believe in free will, in the perfectibility of mankind, in the ability of people to make the right choices, do good, and make things better.[63]

The generalization of Pelagianism denied that Adam's sin has any effect upon mankind other than being a bad example. Mankind can do right and live a sinless life if he were to choose to do so.

Not wanting to lose track of the thesis of this book, it must be noted that this is not a writing in defense of Pelagius. There is much to disagree with him about his doctrinal stand on many issues. However, this writing was to show the concept of original sin as interpreted in the Augustinian fashion is a philosophical position that is based upon Roman tradition and general acceptance rather

62. Jennings, *Pelagius*, 9.
63. Axworthy, *Revenge of Pelagius*.

than on Scripture. To disagree with the orthodox Roman ideology is to be automatically placed into the heretical camp of the Pelagians, whether it be the modern version or that of antiquity. It has been shown, that before Augustine, there was a time when original sin was seen as the inherited death of the body and not necessarily the contamination of the spirit.

THE ROMAN CHURCH (COUNCIL OF TRENT 1546 AD)

These essays of Augustine spring the foundational teaching of original sin by the Roman Church. The Roman Church took this teaching to the extreme and placed anathemas upon any who would disagree with them.

> If anyone asserts that the prevarication of Adam injured himself alone, and not his posterity; and that the holiness and justice received of God, which he lost, he lost for himself alone, and not for us also; or that he, being defiled by the sin of disobedience, has only transfused death, and pains of the body, into the whole human race, but not sin also, which is the death of the soul; let him be anathema.[64]

The logical steps to follow from this doctrinal stand would be adherence to the church and its teaching on how to be absolved of this original sinful spirit. This harks back to Augustine's argument with Pelagius and the stated need to allow babies to come to Christ so that they may be saved.

In the first chapter of this book, it is noted that the Roman Church had a tradition of limbo until recent years. Limbo was the place where the unbaptized babies would go at death, along with others who were not deemed to be evil but were not baptized into the Roman Church. The papal bull bears repeating in this chapter in order to trace the concept of original sin and infant salvation.

> Finally, this same holy Synod teaches those little children, who have not attained the use of reason, are not by

---

64. "General Council of Trent: Fifth Session."

> any necessity obliged to the sacramental communion of
> the Eucharist: forasmuch as, having been regenerated by
> the laver of baptism and being incorporated with Christ,
> they cannot, at that age, lose the grace which they have
> already acquired of being the sons of God.[65]

The doctrine of original sin in the early church progressed from being held in little regard by Hebrew scholars and early church fathers to one of major importance in the Roman Church. Major ceremonial practices are instituted on the foundation that infants need salvation because of the inherited corruption of their spirits.

Although Augustine had the ear of the Roman Church hierarchy as well as popular opinion, his doctrines were not universally adopted. However, his teachings on original sin and infant corruption still have a major following today.

REFORMATION CHURCHES

The churches of the reformation took some very bold stands against the Roman Church. Considering the Roman Church controlled most of the governments of Europe and held dominion over most of the populace, it was quite a feat of faith for these champions to stand up against the powers of the time. After a thousand years of the "dark ages," when a study of actual Scriptures was either belittled or denied, it is no wonder that the reformers carried with them some of the traditions and doctrines of the Roman Church. The doctrine of original sin, as described by Augustine, and the need for infant salvation are two of the doctrines that many of the reformers transferred into their new denominations.

THE ANGLICAN CHURCH

When Henry VIII broke from the Roman Church and founded the Church of England, it was necessary to put into official status

---

65. "General Council of Trent: Twenty-First Session."

the beliefs of the new denomination. What started out as The Ten Articles of Religion (1536 AD) ended up being the Thirty-Nine Articles of Religion (1571 AD). These thirty-nine articles remain the focal point of the Anglican and Episcopal Churches and form part of the Book of Common Prayer.

Although separating itself from Rome, the new Church of England kept many of the traditions and doctrines of the Roman religion. On the doctrine of original sin, the Articles state:

IX. Of Original Sin or Birth-Sin

Original sin standeth not in the following of Adam (as the Pelagians do vainly talk), but it is the fault and corruption of the Nature of every man that naturally is engendered of the offspring of Adam, whereby man is very far gone from original righteousness, and is of his own nature inclined to evil so that the flesh lusteth always contrary to the Spirit; and therefore, in every person born into this world, it deserves God's wrath and damnation. And this infection of nature doth remain, yea in them that are regenerated; whereby the lust of the flesh, . . . (which some do expound the wisdom, some sensuality, some the affection, some the desire, of the flesh), is not subject to the Law of God. And although there is no condemnation for them that believe and are baptized; yet the Apostle doth confess, that concupiscence and lust hath of itself the nature of sin.[66]

This text clearly states that every person is deserving of God's damnation from birth. Further, the cure for this state of original sin as well as all personal sin, is baptism for them that believe. The practice of infant baptism is continued in the church, howbeit the reasoning is rather vague.

XXVII. Of Baptism

Baptism is not only a sign of profession, and a mark of difference, whereby Christian men are discerned from others that be not christened, but it is also a sign of

---

66. "Thirty-Nine Articles of Religion."

Regeneration or New-Birth, whereby, as by an instrument, they that receive Baptism rightly are grafted into the Church; the promises of the forgiveness of sin, and of our adoption to be the sons of God by the Holy Ghost, are visibly signed and sealed, Faith is confirmed, and Grace increased by virtue of prayer unto God.

The Baptism of young Children is in any wise to be retained in the Church, as most agreeable with the institution of Christ.[67]

Although one is able to find various expositions for the doctrine within the theology circles of the Anglican Church, suffice it to say the authority of the Articles found it necessary to continue the practice of infant baptism, which many have come to accept as infant salvation.

THE LUTHERAN CHURCH

Martin Luther's revolutionary reformation movement changed much in the entire Western civilization. His vitriolic attack on all popish persons is quite famous or infamous, and he is quoted by Bible scholars as well as Adolf Hitler.[68] A close look at Martin Luther's doctrine can be quite eye-popping on some subjects.

Regarding original sin, the Lutheran denomination gives a lengthy explanation of its stance in the Book of Concord. The Book of Concord (1580 AD) has remained the official statement of the doctrine of the Lutheran Church. "That this hereditary evil is the guilt [by which it comes to pass] that, by reason of the disobedience of Adam and Eve, we are all in God's displeasure, and by nature children of wrath, as the apostle shows."[69]

In keeping with the adamant views of Luther, any dissenting view is quickly banished but erroneously said to be part of the known heresies of the day, these being the Pelagians and the Manicheans. "Now this doctrine must be so maintained and guarded

67. "Thirty-Nine Articles of Religion."
68. Olsen, "Luther and Hitler."
69. "Formula of Concord ~ Solid Declaration."

that it may not deflect either to the Pelagian or the Manichean side."[70] There is no room to disagree and be considered biblical in their eyes. The Missouri Synod of the Lutheran Church continues the legacy of original sin and paedobaptism in their writings. Their doctrine would show the necessity of infant baptism to wash away the original sin of Adam.

> Terms the Bible uses to talk about the beginning of faith include "conversion" and "regeneration." Although we do not claim to understand fully how this happens, we believe that when an infant is baptized, God creates faith in the heart of that infant.
>
> We believe this because the Bible says that infants can believe (Matt. 18:6) and that new birth (regeneration) happens in Baptism (John 3:5–7; Titus 3:5–6). The infant's faith cannot yet, of course, be verbally expressed or articulated by the child, yet it is real and present all the same (see, e.g., Acts 2:38–39; Luke 1:15; 2 Tim. 3:15).[71]

These two examples, Anglican and Lutheran, serve as an example of Protestant high church doctrine. Low church doctrinal examples will include Methodists and Baptists. The low church denomination examples are more difficult to pin down on any particular doctrine as they are usually made up of various independent churches without a central body mandating local church beliefs.

THE METHODIST CHURCH

The Methodist movement was founded by John and Charles Wesley, as well as others. It became a denomination after the death of John Wesley. In John Wesley's sermon on original sin, he compares Christianity with any type of Heathenism.

> This, therefore, is the first grand distinguishing point between Heathenism and Christianity. The one

---

70. "Formula of Concord ~ Solid Declaration."
71. "FAQs about Doctrine."

acknowledges that many men are infected with many vices, and even born with a proneness to them; but supposes withal, that in some the natural good much over-balances the evil: The other declares that all men are conceived in sin," and "shapen in wickedness;"—that hence there is in every man a "carnal mind, which is enmity against God, which is not, cannot be, subject to" his "law;" and which so infects the whole soul, that "there dwelleth in" him, "in his flesh," in his natural state, "no good thing;" but "every imagination of the thoughts of his heart is evil," only evil, and that "continually."[72]

Wesley, like others, gives no room for disagreement, and blatantly states that anyone who would disagree is a heathen. "Allow this, and you are so far a Christian. Deny it, and you are but a Heathen still."[73]

A United Methodist handbook of doctrine, *By Water and the Spirit: A United Methodist Understanding of Baptism*, records the thoughts of John Wesley in regard to infant baptism and salvation.

Within the Methodist tradition, baptism has long been a subject of much concern, even controversy. John Wesley retained the sacramental theology which he received from his Anglican heritage. He taught that in baptism, a child was cleansed of the guilt of original sin, initiated into the covenant with God, admitted into the Church, made an heir of the divine kingdom, and spiritually born anew. He said that while baptism was neither essential nor sufficient for salvation, it was the "ordinary means" that God designated for applying the benefits of the work of Christ in human lives.

On the other hand, although he affirmed the regenerating grace of infant baptism, he also insisted upon the necessity of adult conversion for those who have fallen from grace.[74]

---

72. Wesley, *Original Sin*, 3.

73. Wesley, *Original Sin*, 3.

74. "By Water and the Spirit," 1.

To Wesley, original sin in infants is washed away by baptism, but due to the fact that future actions may negate salvation in adults, baptism cannot be said to be the sole sufficiency for salvation.

THE BAPTIST CHURCH

The first recognized denominational Baptist church was founded by John Smyth in 1609 in Amsterdam.[75] Followers of Smyth returned to London and started other Baptist congregations. They rejected the concept of predestination of individual souls for salvation or damnation and were thus called General Baptists. The Particular Baptist followed sometime later. They were referred to as particular due to their acceptance of Calvinistic doctrines that only particular individuals were chosen to be the recipients of God's grace. Baptists congregations have remained independent in their government and theology, so it remains difficult to establish a central ideology of any biblical concept beyond the basic tenants that define a Baptist congregation.

The doctrinal statement of the Southern Baptist Convention is viewed in the book *Baptist Faith and Message*. In this text, original sin is addressed.

> Through the temptation of Satan, man transgressed the command of God and fell from his original innocence, whereby his posterity inherited a nature and an environment inclined toward sin. Therefore, as soon as they are capable of moral action, they become transgressors and are under condemnation.[76]

Although there would be other Baptists that would fully accept original sin as Augustine presented it, the official stand of the Southern Baptist Convention would be that a child is not guilty of sin until the capability to understand sin is in place. Those who would follow the Particular Baptist doctrine would be more inclined to disagree.

---

75. *Oxford Dictionary of the Christian Church*, 129.
76. "Baptist Faith and Message 2000."

In this same source, baptism is addressed. It should be noted with great interest that infant baptism and infant salvation are not topics in writing. "Christian baptism is the immersion of a believer in water in the name of the Father, the Son, and the Holy Spirit. It is an act of obedience symbolizing the believer's faith in a crucified, buried, and risen Savior, the believer's death to sin, the burial of the old life, and the resurrection to walk in the newness of life in Christ Jesus."[77]

It would then seem that if there is no original corruption in the soul of an infant, then the need for infant baptism for salvation is negated entirely. This would lead to a question of what exact knowledge Adam gained by eating the forbidden fruit and if that knowledge was passed down to his descendants. The doctrine of original sin is inherently connected to the knowledge of good and evil, which was imparted by the disobedience of the first parents.

MODERN EVOLUTION OF INFANT SALVATION

Brian H. Butler's essay on "Infant Salvation; An Ecumenical Problem" addresses this issue from a more contemporary stance. Butler states there are three main groups that have taken an interest in this quandary of infant salvation over the last few years.

> The ecumenical perspective has caused Roman Catholic theologians to make fresh inquiries concerning the salvation of non-Roman believers, and this has led to fresh thought on the topic of infants who die unbaptized and also the fate of unbaptized heathen.
>
> Presbyterians . . . The Westminster Confession speaks of 'Elect Infants dying in infancy ...' Are there, then, nonelected infants who die reprobate?
>
> Baptist . . . more appropriate in this connection to denote them by the term antipedobaptists . . . infants dying in infancy would be saved apart from baptism.[78]

77. "Baptist Faith and Message 2000."

78. Butler, *Infant Salvation*, 344–60.

Besides these three main groups, Butler also states that Barthian theology has gained quite a bit of traction in these last few years. This theology rejects the entire concept of the need for salvation and rather adheres to universal salvation for any and all.

Of the three major groups of biblical thought on infant salvation, Butler's paper reduces each concept to its basic lowest denominator. The Roman view is that each child is born with Adam's original sin and spiritual damnation. Therefore, the only way to rid an infant of that sin is through the sacrament of baptism. This does not fully answer the question proposed as to the unbaptized infant.

The Reformed view is based entirely upon the predestination of God for each individual soul. Many of the reformed theologians will state the election of infants and, therefore, their final resting place of heavenly eternity. The logical outcome of this theology is that unelected infants are therefore condemned to the fires of damnation for eternity. This statement is obviously left out of many of the election-based salvation theologies.

The Baptist view, according to Butler, is a divided camp. There are some who hold to the Particular Baptist viewpoint, which would put them in the same classification as the Reformed church. Others are of the General Baptist persuasion and would advocate that all infants are heaven bound. Butler records a paper written by the followers of John Smyth, which was written in their quest to be joined by the Dutch Mennonites.

> 20. That infants are conceived and born in innocence without sin, and that so dying are undoubtedly saved, and that this is to be understood of all infants, under heaven (Gen. V.2; i.27 compared with I Cor. XV.49) for where there is no law there is no transgression, sin is not imputed while there is no law (Rom. iv. 15 and V.13), but the law was not given to infants, but to them that could understand (Rom. v.13; Matt, xiii.9; viii.3).[79]

The argument of the antipedobaptists would be that if there is no original sin in an infant's soul, there is no need for pedobaptism.

---

79. Lumpkin, *Baptist Confessions of Faith*, 127.

Butler concludes his paper by summarizing each of the views and also pointing out what he would deem to be the fallacies of unanswered questions left by each. His essay ends with the statement, "It seems that the best answer is the Zwinglian one: the fact of infant death indicates a special interest by God in the child and is a sign of his electing love. And that leads us inevitably, as does all theology, to our doctrine of God. For us, he is the Father, the Abba of his children whom he delights in gathering at his feet."[80]

PROFILE OF THE CURRENT STUDY

Through the study of the presented literature, a pattern of thought can emerge regarding infant salvation and the guilt associated with original sin. The Barthian type of theology will be excluded due to its negating any need for anyone's salvation. Although this has gained a popular following in the last several years, it will deny the literal interpretation of Scripture.

> There are two ways of dealing with this situation. One is a new form of exegesis of the texts about final condemnation, which acknowledges the note of finality but sees these texts as threats rather than predictions. A threat need not be carried out. This, as we shall see, is the approach adopted by the most persuasive of modern universalists.
>
> The second approach to the exegetical problem is simply to disagree with the NT writers' teaching about a final division of mankind.[81]

Likewise, the theology of Origen is also to be excluded in this summary as he also denies any literal interpretation of the Genesis account.

The redefining of terminology seems to be a practice throughout the review of the literature. Good is often used in the place of righteousness and is equated with God. Evil is seen as always being in conflict with the nature of God and is viewed as

---

80. Butler, *Infant Salvation: An Ecumenical Problem*, 356.

81. Bauckham, "Universalism."

sin. Modern terminology has fared no better. Civil righteousness is either the righteousness of one's own good works, or it is the gift of God given in the gospel. All of this adds to the cloudy theology of the line in the sand that defines whether a soul is guilty in the eyes of God's righteousness or not.

With the Hebrew scholars, ancient and contemporary, their theology concerning children is vague and contradictory. Some would claim an original hereditary sin, while others deny such. The need for circumcision is justified by the original sin passed down from Adam or Eve in some minds, yet it is also said to be cleansed at Mount Sinai. The question of uncircumcised infants is not addressed. The Hebrew scholars, by and large, simply ignore the question of original sin until they are forced to answer, as in the case of the early Christian church pushing the doctrine.

Next, the early church fathers showed the same avoidance of the subject of original sin as did the Hebrew scholars. It did not seem to be a subject of utmost concern until the time of Ambrose and then Augustine. These early church fathers were content to leave the Genesis narrative to the same importance that the other Old Testament writers did, which is to not mention it or to do so in a passing and vague way.

The writings of Augustine were the cement in which the doctrine was encased so that it became a foundation for several of the doctrines of the Roman Church. There are some coincidental occurrences that may need to be considered in the writings of Augustine. His own addiction to sexual pleasure seemed to play a major role in the development of his doctrine. The need to solidify the doctrines and the authoritative voice of the Roman Church became apparent at this time. Augustine was to become the voice of debatable reason for the church, which in turn became the voice of many of the medieval governments. The need to baptize babies to negate the damnation of original sin would rate high on the scale of necessity in an era when infant mortality was at a historical peak.

The Reformation churches continued with the doctrine that original sin is carried by infants. These reformation denominations had to therefore decide some way to include infants in their plan of salvation, and most did so by including pedobaptism in their church doctrines.

The views of each denomination, preacher, and movement concerning infant salvation were predicated on their views of original sin. Those who believed in the taint of sin in an infant's soul were also inclined to believe in infant baptism as a means of washing away that sin of Adam. The churches that adopted a predestination of each soul to be saved or lost would, as often as not, subscribe to pedobaptism. The persons that died in infancy and were not baptized were not chosen by God's grace to be saved. For the anti-pedobaptist, the major reason for abstaining from, or preaching against, infant baptism was the lack of original sin in the spirit of the infant. If there is no original sin in the spirit, then there is no sin to wash away in the infant.

The typology of Adam, not only as a picture of the Second Adam Jesus Christ but as a picture of each person born, is an important one. Adam comes into the world just as a child. He is naked, unashamed, and innocent in mind and heart. Those scholars who dealt with the issue have various opinions on the state and knowledge of Adam before the fall, as well as the purpose of God placing the tree in the Garden. Adam is seen by some of the authors as having been created innocent but not "perfect." He was expected to grow in knowledge and righteousness, just as every child should. Adam obviously tried to take a shortcut to knowledge which led to his sin. This typology places each person born in the same situation. One is born innocent in spirit but must choose to follow God as one matures. Adam could have come to know good and evil without it causing sin or broken fellowship with God. In the stance of the Southern Baptist Convention, it is implied that if one could refrain from sin, they would die in Adam's flesh but would never be condemned as lost. However, no man of mental capability except Christ is able to withstand the temptation, and all succumb to it at some point. Considering this point, would one be able to say a baby was never lost?

Luther and Melanchthon's division of the two types of righteousness may provide more insight into Adam's pre-fall condition. Adam did know of some good and evil, as stated before, but did he understand how that civil good and evil affected his standing with the righteousness of God? That question may be asked concerning the infant, toddler, or young child. Are their comprehension and subsequent violation of the civil righteousness that is expected of them in order to be in harmony with their community enough to condemn their souls to the lake of fire? Are these souls already born under the condemnation of the wrath of God?

As with many of the doctrines of the Bible, denominational preference demands that one's beliefs be placed in one extreme or the other. In the case of original sin, a theologian expects to be in the camp of the Augustinians or the Pelagians. These camps decree that one accept original sin, which condemns the infant, or that there is no such doctrine as original sin in any form. This demand for "one or the other" proves itself to be wrong, as usual.

It is possible to have a disparity between the written aspects of a doctrine and its practical application. The medical field distinguishes between laboratory reports and clinical evaluations because the actual prognosis does not always follow the expected textbook outcome. The same can be true of the ministry. All the literature reviewed in this book does not provide adequate answers to the questions regarding infant mortality and salvation. There may be a difference in the practical aspects of the ministry from the doctrinal statements of a denomination regarding the interaction between the minister and grieving parents.

As part of this project, a questionnaire was sent to a variety of local pastors and churches. The responses were varied but mostly held within the parameters that were set by the traditional statements already recorded. There were a few deviations, but these still did not give a biblical answer to the main question of what happens to the innocent when they die, or even if they are innocent. Due to a privacy clause in the questionnaire, those responses cannot be included in this book.

3

Building the Foundation

THE FOLLOWING PAGES WILL contain discussions of several topics, including the impeccability of Christ, pedobaptism, predestination, and others. Each of these will have relevance to the topic of why the innocent do not go to hell. An in-depth examination of these subject matters is necessary in order to answer the basic questions in a sufficient manner that can be provided in a few paragraphs. These topics are also necessary in order to show a structured flow of theology concerning the generally accepted doctrine of original sin, as stated by Augustine.

THE FIRST BASIC QUESTION

The first basic question is, What is the difference between disobedience and unrighteousness? The general consensus, and one supported by Scripture, is that the fall of Adam into sin brought about a knowledge of good and evil. Genesis 3:22: "And the LORD God said, Behold, the man is become as one of us, to know good and evil: and now, lest he put forth his hand, and also take off the tree of life, and eat, and live forever."

The question that arises is not whether Adam gained a knowledge of good and evil, but what exactly that knowledge was and how it affected him and his descendants. One must consider the admonition that God gave to Adam in order to set this pre-fall theology. Genesis 2:15–17: "And the LORD God took the man, and put him into the garden of Eden to dress it and to keep it. And the LORD God commanded the man, saying, of every tree of the garden thou mayest freely eat: But of the tree of the knowledge of good and evil, thou shalt not eat of it: for in the day that thou eatest thereof thou shalt surely die."

In this warning given by God to Adam, one is able to see some of what Adam already knew before the fall:

First, Adam knew what was described as good. Everything God had created was said to be good in the Genesis chapter 1 account. God is himself given the attribute of good in Ps 34:8, as Scripture states that "the Lord is good." The tree of the knowledge of good and evil could not be said to be Adam's only knowledge of good.

Before he ate of that tree, Adam had a knowledge and sense of the goodness of God. Everything in Adam's world was good. It is generally taught that this tree gave knowledge of evil without much thought or regard to the statement that it is the tree of the knowledge of "good and evil." This tree must have imparted unto Adam another depth of knowledge in the realm of what good is.

Second, Adam would have a knowledge of disobedience before he ate of the forbidden fruit as he was forewarned not to eat thereof. If there was no possibility of Adam's disobedience because of a lack of knowledge, then the warning would be a moot point. To admonish Adam not to do something that would not have entered his mind would be for God to violate his own principles. God cannot be tempted with sin, and neither does God tempt others to sin (Jas 1:13). To answer the question of God's temptation of Abraham (Gen 22:1), one must consider that James is writing of God not tempting anyone to do evil. God may very well tempt any of his saints to do right. God may lead us in such a way that Christians are tempted to walk by faith, which is seen in the lives of many of the Bible persons and compiled in Heb 11.

Adam's Picture of Christ and of the Innocence of Babies

Adam is a type of Christ in the scenario of temptation. The doctrine of the Impeccability of Christ has an extremely negative effect on this typology and also confuses the issue of Adam's knowledge before the fall. The doctrine basically states that since Jesus is God, he could not have chosen to sin, nor could he be tempted to sin. Although, on the surface, it may sound like a good doctrine, there is a need to examine this doctrine briefly in order to understand its impact on the typology of Adam and the knowledge held by young children.

It must be emphatically understood by the reader that the demand of Christianity is to believe the Lord Jesus Christ did not commit sin in any form. Jesus Christ did not commit sin in thought, word, or deed. Hebrews 4:15 could not be true if Christ sinned. It states, "For we have not an high priest which cannot be touched with the feeling of our infirmities; but was in all points tempted like as we are, yet without sin." To disagree with that statement is to deny the faith, to blaspheme God with a charge of sin, and to negate the authority and veracity of Scripture. Jesus Christ could not be the vicarious atonement for human sins if he was sinful in himself. First Peter 3:18 states that Jesus is the "just." "For Christ also hath once suffered for sins, the just for the unjust, that he might bring us to God, being put to death in the flesh, but quickened by the Spirit." The question is not "did Jesus Christ sin?" but rather "could Jesus Christ have chosen to sin?"

This doctrine is seen as a biblical statement by some who rest in the knowledge and scriptural fact that God cannot sin (Titus 1:2), neither can he be tempted (Jas 1:13). The problem observed with this philosophical position is that these passages are references to God in his glory, not in a human form (Phil 2:7).

Although God does invite us to "reason" together with him (Isa 1:18), that does not give us the authority to make the word of God subject to human "rationale." Rationale and philosophy open the gateway to speculation, which can result in false doctrine. Most of the cults will take a scriptural truth, add the ingredients of their speculation, and end up with a half-baked idea with which they build their doctrines. The Watchtower Society took the biblical truth of John 1:1 along with the ideas of the Nestorians, added one word to the verse, and came up with Jesus being "a" God. The Church of the Latter-Day Saints took the Bible verse about being baptized for the dead (1 Cor 15:29) and added their twist of being baptized to rescue one's ancestors from hell.[1]

There is no intent or implication to refer to those who believe in the impeccability of Christ as being part of a cult or having cult-like thinking. The examples are given to merely show that rationale cannot be the authoritative method of interpreting Scripture.

In the rationale of accepting the impeccability of Christ, there is a denial of the voluntary limiting that Jesus Christ took upon himself in his incarnation. Hebrews 5:8 is very plain that Jesus learned obedience by the things which he suffered. The prayer of Christ in the garden shows his willingness to do the will of the Father, but it also shows the choice of Christ to follow that will (Luke 22:42). This philosophical approach is that Jesus is God manifest in the flesh, so therefore, all the attributes of God in glory are reflected and imbued upon Jesus Christ as he is incarnate. This will not be a realistic approach to the incarnation of Christ according to Scripture.

The answer for many on the impeccability of Christ is to refer to these two verses: "God cannot be tempted with evil" (Jas 1:13); "it is impossible for God to lie" (Heb. 6:18). The problem arises when one tries to apply these attributes of God in glory to the incarnate Christ.

The questions one must ask are:

a. How does God get hungry? – Luke 4:2

b. How does God not know? – Mark 11:13

c. How does God "become" sin for us? – 2 Cor 5:21

d. How does God "become" a curse for us? – Gal 3:13

e. How does God die? – Rom 5:8

---

1. "Baptism for the Dead."

The context of Heb 13:8, "Jesus Christ the same yesterday, and today, and forever," is defined in the verse which follows that statement. Hebrews 13:9: "Be not carried about with divers and strange doctrines." The doctrines of Jesus Christ, the purpose and the plan, never change. He is not going to bring about some new thing to change everything after the fulfillment of the New Testament. This gives rise to Paul's warnings about even an angel from heaven giving us some new direction (Gal 1:8–9). Joseph Smith would have done well to take heed of these verses when the angel presented himself.[2]

One would need to perform linguistic gymnastics in order to dispel the wording of 2 Cor 5:21. "He became sin for us" is quite clear in its reading as well as correlating with Gal 3:13. This would also explain one of the odd typologies of the Old Testament. In Num 21, Moses was commanded to make a serpent of brass and put it on a pole. The people of Israel were then told to look and live when they were bitten by the deadly fiery serpents. This is a typology of the Lord Jesus Christ as stated in John 3:14: "And as Moses lifted up the serpent in the wilderness, even so, must the Son of man be lifted up."

The serpents mentioned in Scripture are almost always a reference to sin and Satan. Yet, this one is a reference to the Lord Jesus Christ. The explanation is that this is referring to Christ as he became a sin for us on Calvary's cross. Psalm 22 records the forsaking by God the Father of Jesus Christ. Again, God forsook Jesus for a brief time as Jesus became a curse. The cup Jesus prayed to pass from him while he was in the garden is the cup of sin (Matt 26:39). Jesus Christ would have no fear of death as he is the creator of heaven itself and knows what is beyond this mortal life. However, he would have no desire to become sin. It is beyond human imagination to understand the heartache of Jesus Christ as he laid aside his holiness to become every evil and wicked thought, deed, and word that mankind has ever brought upon this earth.

In light of this scriptural truth, it must be noted that Jesus Christ limited himself to the point that he could become sin. It

2. "Angel Moroni."

would not be unreasonable to also assume that Jesus Christ could have chosen to sin while in that mortal flesh.

Jesus Christ made several Old Testament appearances in the bodily form before the incarnation of the virgin birth. If this is a truth, then why the need for a virgin birth? Jesus could have just come to earth at any time in the form of a man. The answer will be found in 1 Cor 15:40. There is celestial flesh and terrestrial flesh. The body of the celestial is immortal and incorruptible (1 Cor 15:53). It cannot die, it cannot sin, and it cannot suffer in any form or fashion. The predestination of the saints is to be conformed to the image of Jesus in glory (Rom 8:29). As we bear the image of the terrestrial Adam now, we will bear the image of the glorified celestial Jesus (1 Cor 15:49). The virgin birth was needed to provide a body for Christ that could suffer, could die, and could refuse the temptations of the choices of sin.

The virgin birth of the Lord Jesus Christ cannot be regarded as a separate doctrinal issue from the main body of the doctrine of Christ. This virgin birth is an integral part of not only the perfect vicarious sacrifice by Jesus but it is also the explanation for how God, when manifest in the flesh, is able to suffer and die for mankind.

The importance of this doctrine is a major component of understanding the birth of Adam's descendants. Adam was created in innocence and yet had the ability to make choices, and he chose to sin. Jesus Christ was born with Adam's flesh but not with Adam's fallen spirit. Jesus had the ability to choose to follow his flesh or to follow his spirit. All of mankind would follow that same pattern. Every person is born of Adam's flesh but with a clean and living spirit. The difference is that when Jesus was presented with the temptations of sin, he chose to reject them. The rest of mankind that has the capacity to understand will eventually give in to the temptations and subsequently will die in their spirit the moment they do so.

As a quick note, let me interject that the doctrine of Traducianism will not hold up to Scripture or reason. This doctrine teaches that nothing new is ever created, so mankind must get their spirits from their parents. If this is true, it raises the question of how a baby has a sinful spirit if its parents were both redeemed with born-again spirits. Scripturally, the answer is given in Eccl 12:7, which states that the "spirit shall return unto God who gave it." God gives each new life a new spirit.

Mankind will begin their spiritual condemnation by making the choice to follow their flesh. This is the context of Rom 7:9 and then Rom 8:1. Once their spirit has died within them, the need to be born again is present (John 3:7). After the new birth, the battle begins again. The saints have to constantly make the choice of listening to their flesh or their spirit as they speak contrary to one another (Gal 5:17). The blessing is that after the new birth, the spirit is no longer contaminated by the sins of the flesh (Col 2:11).

Along with Adam's understanding of what constituted disobedience, Adam would also know the consequences of that disobedience. God informed Adam that if he ate the fruit, he would die. Considering that this is a conversation with God, there is no reason to believe that God is giving Adam warnings of things that he could not possibly conceive the concept.

Adam was given the task of dressing and keeping the garden. It is not usually thought that anything would actually die in that perfect paradise of Eden, but one must consider nature and the natural process of maturing in the animal and plant kingdoms. The curse on nature from the fall of Adam is that the world would bring forth thorns and thistles and that he would return to the dust of the earth. The curse does not mention the death of animal or plant life, so it would be possible that those processes already took place.

Genesis 3:17–19: "And unto Adam, he said, Because thou hast hearkened unto the voice of thy wife, and hast eaten of the tree, of which I commanded thee, saying, Thou shalt not eat of it: cursed *is* the ground for thy sake; in sorrow shalt, thou eat *of* it all the days of thy life; Thorns also and thistles shall it bring forth to thee; and thou shalt eat the herb of the field; In the sweat of thy face shalt thou eat bread, till thou return unto the ground; for out of it was thou taken: for dust thou *art*, and unto dust shalt thou return."

The curse of death was placed upon mankind. There is no scriptural reason to believe that death was not a part of nature, even in paradise. The trees that bore fruit would have also born blossom, which would die to give place to the fruit. The fruit would eventually die and fall from the trees. The animals were a separate creation from man and would not be exempt from dying. This would be the whole point of God giving Adam the occupation of dressing and keeping the garden. Otherwise, there would have been nothing for Adam to accomplish. For God to warn Adam of impending death in regard to himself would have been easily understood by a man who saw death as part of the normal cycle of nature. Adam would have also understood that he was above that nature and therefore given the mandate by the Creator to subdue it as well as have dominion over it (Gen 1:28).

Righteousness is More than Good

It is obvious that partaking of the tree of knowledge of good and evil imparted a specific knowledge to Adam that he did not possess before eating the forbidden fruit. There is a different aspect of "good" that is above and beyond the basic conception. This concept is the righteousness of good.

In much of theology today, good is equated with righteousness. That presents a major obstacle in the minds of many who would try to justify their own thoughts with those of God. What is good or evil in the eyes of society does not necessarily measure up to the definitions of righteous or unrighteous.

In this modern society, these changes in definitions can have a devastating effect while posing as godliness. This is the deception of Satan and his angels, as described in 2 Cor 11. When one takes the moral high road to condemn righteousness, there seems to be little chance of debate, persuasion, or reasoning with that person. Their feeling of moral superiority makes them impervious to the light of Scripture reaching their conscience as one who has seared their conscience with a hot iron. This applies to their understanding of the Scriptures, their defense of heinous acts such as abortion, or their ability to be corrected in any manner of spiritual or social situations. Their humanistic morality gives them the right to decide what is righteous. When this happens, they often find themselves fighting against the God of Righteousness and Morality. John 16:2: "They shall put you out of the synagogues: yea, the time cometh, that whosoever killeth you will think that he doeth God service."

In biblical scenarios, righteousness defines whether good or evil is of God or the devil. The devil can appear as an angel of light (2 Cor 11:14). This would make his appearance seem like a good thing to the people who are flattered by his words (Dan 11:32). Satan also has ministers who portray righteousness but lack that which comes from God (2 Cor 11:15). Following this vein of thought, Eve saw the good in the forbidden fruit (Gen 3:6) and consequently set the whole world on a course of hell. Peter spoke out of a good love for his friend, Jesus, when he stated that he would not let the Lord die (Matt 16:22–23). Jesus's answer to Peter revealed to all that Satan was behind that emotional response. The girl who grieved Paul by her following him and proclaiming to all that Paul had the words of the living God was actually saying good things (Acts 16:16–18). The problem was that she never repented of her unclean spirit and sought to combine her spirit of divination with the name of Jesus Christ.

Society has picked up this trend and seeks to find the good in whatever they want to do. They possess the mindset that if they can find a good point, then it also becomes a righteous point. To try to declare that a genetic boy is really a girl because he feels like such is said to be good because it makes the boy happy for the moment. Abortion is good because it solves the immediate problems that a young girl might face in an unwanted pregnancy. However, there is no righteousness within the parameters of these ideologies. Finding a good did not make these things right.

The concept of evil can be even more daunting when one understands that evil can be righteous if used by God. Exodus 32:14: "And the LORD repented of the evil which he thought to do unto his people." God was going to do evil unto the children of Israel.

The Oxford Dictionary defines evil in a way that fits the context of Exodus by stating that evil is "Something harmful or undesirable."[3]

God can cause harm or something that is undesirable, but he is always righteous in doing so. Abraham asked, "shall not the judge of all the earth do right?" (Gen 18:25). The answer to that question is always yes, and God was totally right in the destruction of Sodom. This same theology is applied to God bringing harm to those who drowned in the flood of Noah and were slaughtered in the occupations recorded in the Chronicles of the Kings, Isaiah, Jeremiah, and the Lamentations. Jesus will righteously judge and make war at the Second Advent (Rev 19:11), while the lake of fire will be the righteous eternal torment of those whose names are not in the book of life (Rev 20:15).

Many can understand the concept of the righteous judgment and condemnation of God, yet they struggle when the actual word "evil" is applied to the actions of God. These same people would also struggle with the realization that good is not always righteous.

It can even be further complicated in the eyes of man because God takes into consideration the heart or motive (1 Sam 16:7). This is the purpose of Rom 8:28. The promise is given to those who are trying to do the will of God. If one is attempting the will of God, they are still able to make a mistake. Paul demonstrates this when he goes to Jerusalem after being repeatedly warned not to do so in the Book of Acts. However, Paul's motive was good (Rom 9:3), and therefore, God worked it out for Paul to end up in Rome as he was commissioned. A person can make a bad decision while trying to serve God and still be counted righteous in their actions.

The Realization of Righteousness in Adam and Children as They Mature

Adam was now able to realize that he violated the natural law of righteousness. In the same way, a toddler knows that a parent has instructed them not to touch something; Adam knew his Father

---

3. *Oxford English Dictionary*, 314.

had given him instructions not to eat the forbidden fruit. Since doing so, Adam's eyes were opened, and the violation of righteousness has become a reality. Adam has instantly matured beyond the reasoning of a toddler. He has not only succumbed to disobedience, but he crossed the line of unrighteousness. Adam now has the knowledge that he has lost the righteousness with which he was clothed (Gen 2:25; Gen 3:7).

In writing for the Westminster Biblical Journal, William N. Wilder states a supposition that God intended for Adam to eventually have the knowledge of good and evil that the tree would impart:

> . . . there is reason to believe that this tree might have played a role in a very different sort of transformation had Adam and Eve only obeyed their sovereign lord (sic). In this case, the opening of their eyes and acquisition of wisdom—their illumination—would have led to a very different outcome. Rather than servicing as the means of their downfall, it would have served as the means of their exaltation—to the righteousness, power, and glory God intended them to enjoy on their viceregal thrones.[4]

Possessing that knowledge of good and evil is not a sin. The Scripture records God the Father saying that Adam has "become as one of us, to know good and evil" (Gen 3:22). The Trinity of God knows good and evil and he is righteous. Just doing good or evil is not necessarily the problem. A young toddler can cause harm by destroying something valuable they were told not to touch, but they are not unrighteous in the heart. Others can do good, and it does not solve their need for salvation, as seen in the case of the rich young ruler (Luke 18:18–23).

Adam's gained knowledge of good and evil is a knowledge of the righteousness of good and evil. He understood more than disobedience and judgment. Now, Adam understands that he has violated the righteousness of God, and he has become unclean, not only in his actions but also in his being.

---

4. Wilder, *Illumination and Investiture*, 52.

THE SECOND BASIC QUESTION

The second basic question is, How did Adam's sin affect all of mankind?

Adam is the human father of all of mankind. His name was given by God on the day he was created (Gen 5:2). Adam's name becomes the Hebrew word for "man," the human species. Adam is also a typology of Jesus Christ, as recorded in 1 Cor 15:45. This typology can even be made to cover the death of Christ. Adam was not deceived as Eve was (1 Tim 2:14) but willingly chose to die with his wife. Jesus Christ also died to be with his bride (Eph 5:25), albeit with a totally different outcome (Gal 2:20). God's reference to Adam and Eve as both being called Adam, or mankind (Gen 5:2), would imply that Adam is also a type of all mankind. Adam was made in the image of God, but Adam's descendants were born in the image of Adam (Gen 5:3).

Humanity seems to follow the steps of this first Adam. One must step away from the traditional doctrine of Augustine's original sin in order to see this typology; however, Scripture will suffice as its authority upon which to build.

Each person is conceived in the image of Adam (Gen 5:3). Humanity lost the divine image of God in that persons are born with Adam's flesh and sin. Romans 5:12 states, "Wherefore, as by one man sin entered into the world, and death by sin; and so, death passed upon all men, for that all have sinned." This is the pivotal verse upon which Augustine's original sin doctrine would hang. To deny that Adam's sin influenced all of mankind would be to deny the clear statement of this verse. The question is not "if" the sin of Adam affected mankind, but "how" the sin of Adam affected mankind.

The context of each verse associated with Adam's sin is in regard to mankind's flesh. There is a very distinct passage of Scripture in Rom 7 that explains the predicament of humanity with Adam's sin upon us. Romans 7:9 records the apostle Paul's message stating, "For I was alive without the law once: but when the commandment came, sin revived, and I died."

Considering Rom 7:9 brings into light of understanding some of the other passages containing a pertinence to this subject. Paul uses the personal pronoun. He was alive without the law, not mankind, but himself. Yet when the commandment of God came to his understanding, he was made aware of the unrighteousness of his actions, and he then died. Following the typology of Adam will fit this dialogue. Adam was innocent in his condition, heart, and mind. But his sin made him aware of God's righteousness and his own failure to uphold that standard. Paul states that awareness also happens in each member of the human race, wherein they also realize the righteousness of God. That moment is when the commandment comes to us. After that realization of God's righteousness is made known and one still chooses to violate that righteousness, then the spirit dies within them.

The passage of Eph 2:1, which declares people to be "dead in trespasses and sins," is written to those whom God "hath quickened." It is a doctrinal statement regarding people who have the intellectual capacity to receive Christ as Savior. This quickening happens after they have believed, as stated emphatically in Eph 1:13: "In whom ye also trusted, after that, ye heard the word of truth, the gospel of your salvation; in whom also after that ye have believed, ye were sealed with the Holy Spirit of promise." The quickening of Eph 2:1 is dependent upon the receiving of Jesus as recorded in John 1:12: "But as many as received Him, to them gave The power to become the sons of God, even to them that believe on His name." The point here is that each of the Scriptures declaring mankind to be under the spiritual damnation of God is directed at those who are able to make the choice of following righteousness or not.

Following this doctrinal line of interpretation in Rom 7:9 will then fit in theology for all of mankind. As Job bemoans the evil that has fallen upon him, he makes a statement of dying as an unborn child. Job 3:11: "Why died I not from the womb? Why did I not give up the ghost when I came out of the belly?" Job makes another declaration of this sort in Job 10:18: "Wherefore then hast thou brought me forth out of the womb? Oh, that I had given up the ghost, and no eye had seen me." Job's doctrine, which God never corrected, was that Job was a living spirit at the time of his infancy, even his yet unborn infancy.

Continuing this line of thought will bring us to two more examples of the untainted spirit within an infant. Jeremiah was recognized as a living person before he actually emerged from the womb (Jer 1:5). It is also recorded that King David lost his son while the boy was still a baby. After the death of the child, David is asked why he stopped grieving. His answer is that ". . . I shall go to him, but he shall not return to me" (2 Sam 12:23). Jeremiah was sanctified by God as a baby, and King David had confidence that his baby boy was with God. This could easily be done if babies have clean spirits at conception.

Jesus Christ seems to confirm this doctrine in Luke 18. As the disciples forbid the parents to bring their children to Jesus, Jesus stops the disciples with the admonition that these children are the kingdom of God (Luke 18:16). This is not just the idea of grown men believing and becoming children in the faith as is commonly taught. This declaration of Christ is the affirmation that the innocent, clean, and living spirit of those children is a part of the kingdom of God. The kingdom of God is a spiritual kingdom (Rom 14:17) that is not made up of physical things at this time, which means the spirit of each little child is part of that kingdom.

Paul's statement in Rom 7:9 concerning his death at the realization of the commandment and righteousness of God is further confirmed by Rom 5:13. After making the authoritative declaration of the guilt of mankind in Adam, Paul's very next sentence is to exclude those who cannot understand that righteousness. Romans 5:13: "For until the law sin was in the world: but sin is not imputed when there is no law." There is no imputation or accounting of sin to those who cannot understand the righteousness of God, which is the law. Paul further excludes these innocents in verse 14 of the passage with the clause, "Nevertheless death reigned from Adam to Moses, even over them that had not sinned after the similitude of Adam's transgression . . ." There are two separate deaths in the passage. The death of the flesh because of Adam's sin and the death of the spirit because of one's own sin.

Although a baby is born with a living and clean spirit, it still has the capability of dying because of inheriting Adam's flesh. As stated in Rom 5:14, earthly, fleshly death reigned upon everyone, even those who did not choose to sin as Adam did. The omniscient God of the Bible has written very clearly that the only persons who would choose not to sin are the Lord Jesus Christ (Heb 4:15) and those who cannot make that choice. This is seen in the statement of Rom 3:23: "For all have sinned and come short of the glory of God." Everyone who can make the choice to sin will eventually do so, although some more than others.

Adam's typology is specific concerning the human race. A baby is born with a soul, a living spirit, and Adam's flesh. This trinity of man is seen in the blessing of Paul as he writes to the Thessalonians: "and the very God of peace sanctify you wholly; and I pray God your whole spirit and soul and body be preserved blameless unto the coming of our Lord Jesus Christ." Paul's statement clarifies the meaning of Gen 1:26, wherein God declares that mankind is to be made in the image of the Triune God, not a heavenly council.

Humanity is born with that trinity of being intact, yet he also has a predilection to sin. The toddler, as Adam did, knows and understands the idea of "do not touch." That young child does not understand that disobeying will result in violating the righteousness of God's laws. Adam is the typology of every toddler. They walk naked with no shame and have trouble putting things in their mouths that were specifically forbidden.

Typologies are never an exact match as they are pictures. The typology of Adam to the rest of humanity differs in that mankind is already born with sinful flesh, as seen in Rom 5:12. This gives mankind a predilection to sin that Adam did not have. The exact similarity is not regarding Adam's flesh, which humanity is born with, but to the spirit within that each person possesses. Adam and Eve died spiritually the moment they ate the forbidden fruit. Each human also dies spiritually when they violate the law of righteousness which God has placed in their conscience.

Humanity develops knowledge of obedience very quickly, but that knowledge is much like Adam's knowledge before the fall. This is seen in the teaching of obedience to the young child. The understanding of righteousness comes with the maturity of the conscience. This natural law of righteousness is a confirmation that there is a righteous God, and the universe operates on a basic righteousness that is cognizant of all of mankind. Romans 2:15: "Which shew the work of the law written in their hearts, their conscience also bearing witness, and their thoughts the mean while accusing or else excusing one another." To understand this knowledge of the law of righteousness is to possess the knowledge of Adam after the fall.

THE THIRD BASIC QUESTION

The third basic question is, Does Adam's sin automatically condemn every human to a judgment of hell? As noted in the chapter on the literature review, the letter of the law for many denominations is to condemn certain infants in condemnation for sin. As this is a most unpalatable circumstance for many today, the same denominations try to find ways of excluding these innocents from the damnation while still maintaining the Augustinian view of original sin. To accomplish this, one must step away from the authority of Scripture alone and accept the authority of tradition and church dogma.

The following paragraphs are an example of how tradition and church dogma try to answer the question of infant salvation. The prevalent answer is seen in infant baptism. The problem is that there is no Scripture to back this claim.

The Tradition of Pedobaptism

Pedobaptism is one of the traditional means of a church attempting to compensate for the Augustinian doctrine. One may argue that the original intent of pedobaptism was to include the children in the community of the congregation while not declaring them to be saved from condemnation because of the baptism. This tradition of infant baptism tends to evolve into infant salvation in the minds of many of the congregants. The apostle Paul made a concise statement that left water baptism out of the gospel in this gentile age of the church.

First Corinthians 15:1–4: "Moreover, brethren, I declare unto you the gospel which I preached unto you, which also ye have received, and wherein ye stand; By which also ye are saved, if ye keep in memory what I preached unto you unless ye have believed in vain. For I delivered unto you first of all that which I also received, how that Christ died for our sins according to the scriptures; And that he was buried, and that he rose again the third day according to the scriptures."

Paul writes again of baptism by stating that he is thankful he did not baptize very many in 1 Cor 1:14. If water baptism were an element of salvation, Paul would not be thanking God that he did not baptize people.

The doctrine of pedobaptism has no actual biblical examples or descriptions. Baptism is part of the Great Commission given to the saints by the resurrected Lord Jesus Christ (Matt 28:19–20). Note that the command to baptize was preceded by the command to teach. The converts would need to be taught first before they are baptized. This is not possible with infant baptism. Every example of specific people being baptized in the Scriptures is always an adult that has accepted the conversion.

Considering the Scripture as the only authority will give an entirely different view of baptism than what is traditionally accepted. The baptism of salvation in the gentile Church Age is seen in Rom 6. The element of this baptism is not water but the Lord Jesus Christ, as stated in verse 3. This is in accordance with the statement of salvation in Gal 2:20: "I am crucified with Christ. Nevertheless, I live . . ." John the Baptist foretold of this spiritual baptism in his statement that when Jesus does appear, there will be additional baptisms, those of the Holy Ghost and fire (Matt 3:11).

The typology of baptism is that of death, burial, and resurrection, as seen in Rom 6:3–4: "Know ye not, that so many of us as were baptized into Jesus Christ were baptized into his death? Therefore, we are buried with him by baptism into death: that like as Christ was raised up from the dead by the glory of the Father, even so, we also should walk in newness of life." The water baptism of the gentile church age is a picture of that spiritual baptism. Water baptism is only a picture is the reason it is not included in the plan of salvation for the church today.

If one does not accept the Augustinian view of original sin and does accept that a child is born with Adam's flesh and a living spirit (Rom 7:9), then this negates the whole concept of pedobaptism. A child's spirit is not dead and, therefore, does not need salvation. The typology of baptism is also lost in infant baptism, as they are not dead in sin and would have no need of a burial and resurrection yet.

Romans 5:12 seems to be the foundational statement of condemning the spirit of infants to the judgment of God. "Wherefore, as by one man sin entered into the world, and death by sin; and so, death passed upon all men, for that all have sinned:" Romans 5:13 should be a foundational statement as well, in that it relieves these innocents from the condemnation that comes from committing sin. "For until the law sin was in the world: but sin is not imputed when there is no law." Once an acceptance of Augustine's original sin has been made, there remain no scriptural means to bypass that judgment in the case of those who are mentally incapable of realizing the gospel or the laws of righteousness.

The Answer to Predestinated Salvation

As a former student who swallowed the teaching of Calvinism, I can say from experience that the idea of being predestined gives no comfort or assurance. Being a student that was required by the Bible College to go evangelizing each week was hard to reconcile with the teaching in the same college that everyone was predestined to heaven or hell.

The problem became so conflicting to me that I would go on visitation and tell folks how they could be saved and then return to the dorm and cry myself to sleep, begging God to let me know that I was one of the chosen. That was the catalyst that provoked my desire for biblical answers and to spend these many years seeking Bible knowledge. I am very pleased to say God provided those answers once I accepted the Bible as my final authority.

I cannot imagine the turmoil in a parent's heart, if they have lost a child, to not have the assurance that their baby is in heaven. But, if one accepts the doctrine of Calvinism, there is no Scripture that guarantees that you are one of the chosen, much less your spouse or your children. To get around this, Calvinists came up with the doctrine that if you are saved, then your children are automatically as well. So, one only has to find an ancestor that is redeemed, and then everyone down the line would be as well. Calvinism fails miserably in every aspect of Bible proof, comfort, and reason. Calvinism would put millions of innocents in hell because they were not chosen.

4

Answering the Question

THERE MUST BE A defined line between innocence and guilt in order to minister to the loved ones of a deceased child. To give empty platitudes is equal to deception. A minister must be equipped to engage with the parents and loved ones who have suffered this loss, as it is certainly going to happen in their long-term ministry. Mental disability is a not-so-rare condition of birth defects or accidents. Infant mortality may be much less than what it was years ago. However, it still happens and will most likely be encountered by any minister who remains in their calling for a very long.

The main question is, How do we know these innocents go to heaven, and what is the line in the sand that makes a person guilty in the judgment of God? God has always given the scripturally detailed mechanics of the doctrines one must use to minister to others. This is the command Paul gives to Timothy in order to see the continuance of the ministry beyond their personal work. Second Timothy 2:2: "And the things that thou hast heard of me among many witnesses, the same commit thou to faithful men, who shall be able to teach others also." This main question must be answered in a biblical manner that can find its roots in the creation of Adam and be followed to the present time.

THE CREATION OF ADAM

The narration of Gen 1:26 describes the creation of the first human to be in the image of God. The image that humanity was modeled after was the image of the Holy Trinity: God the Father, God the Son, and God the Holy Spirit. Mankind is the only being of the creation that is also a trinity in and of himself.

The doctrine of the Trinity of God is extremely important to the understanding of the salvation of mankind in general and the salvation of babies and innocent adults in particular. In order to comprehend the separation between the spiritual makeup of humanity (soul and spirit) and the physical elements of humanity (the body), one must have a basic understanding of the image upon which mankind was created. The Trinitarian doctrine has been disputed for ages, as seen in the history of the Arians, which begat the modern-day Watchtower Society.

Not only does one need to recognize the Triune Being of God as one Lord (Deut 6:4) but also the distinct separation of those three entities. Again, this is necessary for understanding the image from which mankind was fashioned. As the Holy Trinity has separate roles,[1] so too the trinity of man has distinct and separate qualities. In God's trinity, the Father has the role of directing and will (John 3:16; 2 Pet 3:9). God the Son has the role of Redeemer (Acts 4:12; John 14:6). God the Holy Spirit has the purpose of regenerating (Titus 3:5).

The apostle Paul affirms the doctrine of the Trinity of God and mankind's being made in that likeness when he writes to the Thessalonians and states, "And the very God of peace, sanctify you wholly; and I pray God your whole spirit and soul and body be preserved blameless unto the coming of our Lord Jesus Christ" (1 Thess 5:23). The author of the epistle to the Hebrews also describes this trinity of mankind when writing in Heb 4:12, "For the word of God is quick, and powerful, and sharper than any two-edged sword, piercing even to the dividing asunder of soul and spirit, and of the joints and marrow, and is a discerner of the thoughts and

---

1. Flowers, "Theology II TH804."

intents of the heart." The three parts of the being of man are seen in the mention of soul, spirit, and physical body elements. This separates the creation of mankind from all other beings.

Adam's creation has a component of knowledge that includes an immature realization of good and evil. That knowledge is not fully developed. God bestowed this knowledge in enough measure that Adam could understand the concepts of God's admonition to not eat of the tree of good and evil. Adam was able to understand the command and the choice. He was able to comprehend the warning of disobedience, the judgment of disobedience, and the penalty of disobedience.

The statement of God, "Behold the man has become like one of us, to know good and evil" (Gen 3:22), is a clear indication of knowledge in holiness. God, in his holiness and righteousness, knows good and evil to its fullest extent, and yet he remains holy and righteous. To realize that Adam knew the basics of good (obedience) and evil (disobedience and judgment) is no large step. It would seem the plan of God was that as Adam matured, God would instruct him, and he would eventually understand those concepts to a complete level. The tree provided a shortcut to that knowledge without the maturity of righteousness to control it.

This pattern of maturity is repeated in the New Testament in the form of charity. It is often said that charity is defined as love, and the word is often substituted in translations of Scripture. However, charity is more than love. Love is included in the doctrine, but it only describes one aspect of charity.

Charity is listed with faith and hope in 1 Cor 13:13: "And now abide the faith, hope, charity, these three; but the greatest of these is charity." When one considers the demonstrable definitions of these words, the purpose of charity being named as the greatest becomes clearer. Faith believes what God said. It is the foundation of Christianity, and without faith, one cannot please God (Heb 11:6) nor be a partaker of salvation (Eph 2:8–9). Hope is the confident expectation of God's promises. It differs from faith in that faith believes everything God said, including judgments, damnation, and curses. Hope is the positive aspect of faith that gives us the hope of Jesus's promised return (Titus 2:13) and the hope of salvation (Rom 8:24). Hope is the reassurance from God that allows us to endure the temptations and trials of this earthly life.

Charity is learning to walk in the spirit of God. In a common vernacular, charity is growing up. God is love (1 John 4:8), but God is never said to have charity because God in glory never had to grow up. To believe what God said and to have a confident expectation in his promises are necessary for the Christian life. Yet, in immature hands and minds, those two things can be twisted and wrested to the destruction of the bearer. This is the admonition given in Heb 5:14: "But strong meat belonged to them that are of full age, *even* those who by reason of use have their senses exercised to discern both good and evil." The immature will destroy themselves and others with their interpretations of scriptural doctrines, which often end up being taken out of context, as seen in 2 Pet 3:16, "As also in all *his* epistles, speaking in them of these things; in which are some things hard to be understood, which they that are unlearned and unstable wrest, as *they also do* the other scriptures, unto their own destruction."

Eve was tempted by Satan to take a shortcut to this maturity. His words offered a desire to make one wise; Gen 3:5–6: "For God doth know that in the day ye eat thereof, then your eyes shall be opened, and ye shall be as gods, knowing good and evil. And when the woman saw that the tree *was* good for food and that it *was* pleasant to the eyes, and a tree to be desired to make *one* wise, she took of the fruit thereof, and did eat, and also gave unto her husband with her, and he did eat."

Charity is "that which is perfect" (1 Cor 13:10), which, when it comes, no longer has to have the signs and wonders to prove God. This need to validate God's word with physical manifestations becomes evil because of the lack of charity; Matt 12:39: "But he answered and said unto them, an evil and adulterous generation seeketh after a sign; and there shall no sign be given to it, but the sign of the prophet Jonas."

ADAM'S FALL IN SIN

Adam made a choice to die with his wife. This choice cost Adam his innocence and righteous image of the Holy God. Although Adam is still a trinity in his being, his life is no longer in the Spirit of God but is now in his blood. At the creation, God breathed into man the breath of life (Gen 2:7), and he became a living soul. After the fall, God reveals that the life of man is in the blood (Lev 17:11).

One may make the argument that Gen 2:7 refers to the soul of man while Lev 17:11 refers to the flesh. These are Old Testament references, though, which are further expounded upon in the New Testament doctrines. The soul and body (flesh) of a person are connected in the Old Testament and in those unsaved in the New Testament. This is the reasoning behind the warning of "the soul that toucheth shall be unclean" (Num 19:22). Anything that is touched by the flesh will contaminate the soul as well. God gives enough revelation to still realize they are separate entities, as with Rachel dying while giving birth. The Bible clearly states, "as her soul was in departing" (Gen 35:18).

This connection of soul and flesh is a major component of New Testament salvation. To be born again, the spirit of man is born of the Spirit of God (John 3:6). This born-again spirit is birthed of incorruptible seed (1 Pet 1:23) and is thus incapable of sin (1 John 5:18). The dilemma results from the honesty of realizing that after salvation, one still commits sin (1 John 1:8). The question becomes, How does a Christian sin and remain sinless? The answer is found in this connection between the soul and flesh.

The spirit of a man saved is sinless, and the soul is part of that spiritual being. The flesh of a Christian still sins, as Paul so vehemently affirms in Rom 7. The circumcision made without hands is the answer to this riddle. Colossians 2:11 "In whom also ye are circumcised with the circumcision made without hands, in putting off the body of the sins of the flesh by the circumcision of Christ."

Eternal life is restored to the spiritual elements of man (soul and spirit), while the flesh still has its temporal problems and destiny. This explains why the statement of the wages of sin (Rom 6:23) still applies to the saints. The body of a saint still sins and will still meet death if the Lord Jesus tarries.

This discourse of life is lengthy but necessary. It confirms the idea of mankind retaining its inherent trinity of being after the fall and yet still losing the image of God. Adam's descendants no longer had the image of God. They bore the image of Adam, Gen 5:3: "And Adam lived a hundred and thirty years, and begat *a son* in his own likeness, after his image; and called his name Seth." These children bear Adam's sinful flesh, which carries its life in Adam's blood. The spirit of these children will be discussed in later pages, but suffice it to say they have their own spirits. Their flesh gives the inclination to sin that God's image does not possess.

The sin of Adam, born in the flesh of all humanity, leads mankind to face the choices of good and evil. The problem remains the same as with Adam; mankind is faced with this choice without a righteous understanding to complete the picture. Although the conscience will convict one of the consequences (Rom 2:14–15), man lacks a defined understanding of eternal judgment and condemnation for such actions.

Humanity's ignorance of God's righteousness leads them to promote their own righteousness instead (Rom 10:3). They have an inherited knowledge of how to commit sin while also knowing how to excuse the same. What mankind lacks is the knowledge of how to be absolved from that sin; 1 Tim 2:4: "Who will have all men to be saved, and to come unto the knowledge of the truth." Mankind has become a little child who possesses deadly weapons without any maturity of knowing how to handle them. Adam's partaking of the tree of good and evil bestowed upon mankind a knowledge of good and evil beyond his immature innocence while also giving his descendants a flesh that is prone to rebellion and unrighteousness. Therefore, the death of the flesh, the result of the wages of sin, is passed upon to all humanity (Rom 5:12), while the individual spirit still remains innocent until making the choice to sin (Rom 5:13).

BIRTH INTO ADAM'S SIN

There seems to be no question amongst most denominations of Christianity that mankind is born with the curse of Adam's sin upon it. The discussion would then revolve around how the curse affects humanity and the procedure by which to negate the damnation of that curse. Augustine's writings and that of his adherents are vague and contradicting at times. As seen in previous chapters, Augustine seems to finally land on the concept that original sin is passed down from parent to child in the act of procreation, as that act in itself is lustful and, therefore, constitutes a sin. Most of the Augustinian followers would then say a baby is born with a spirit that is dead in trespasses and sins.

The question then left by Augustine's doctrine would be to ask how that infant is then cleansed from Adam's sin. Most would say that pedobaptism is the necessary step of infant salvation; yet again, it would leave the question unanswered as to what happens to unbaptized infants upon their death. According to the literature review, and along with the confirmation of the pastoral survey, this question is largely ignored.

A look at the doctrines of soteriology will reveal not only the plan of salvation but also the mechanics of salvation. The first purpose of Scripture, as recorded in 2 Tim 3:16–17, is "doctrine." God has given detailed accounts of the mechanics of the doctrines of Scripture. Faith is not a blind trust; it believes what God said. The purpose of using blood (Lev 17:11), the law of righteousness (Ezek 18:4), and the vicarious atonement (Heb 9:12) are all explained in detail with the prophecies and typologies of the Old Testament as well as the mechanics of the New Testament. Howbeit, when it comes to infant salvation, it is often seen as an unanswerable mystery that must hope for the best. Augustine's doctrine fails to provide the mechanics of doctrine to answer this mystery.

EVIDENCE OF AN INFANT'S LIVING SPIRIT

The question to be settled before one can begin to comprehend the dilemma of Augustine's doctrine is one of authority. Extra-canonical writings seem to be the acceptable foundation of some theologians and are used to prop up pre-conceived ideas of Adam's sin being passed along to an infant's spirit.

These pseudo-graphical writings also become the basis for some in their quest to allow children into heaven. The heretical Books of Enoch have become popular with some as doctrinal statements to be viewed as a legitimate authority.

Although one may find a nugget of truth in anything, it certainly does not make the whole a truth, nor is it a commendation that the whole is worthy of any consideration.

The evidence of infant salvation is confirmed by Scripture rather than tradition or the extra-canonical books. Second Samuel 11–12 record David's act of adultery with Bathsheba and the baby born from that sinful union. Nathan, the prophet, uses the scenario of a man stealing another man's beloved sheep to confront David for his actions. David's own judgment against this supposed thief is that he would repay fourfold. The principle of "by thy words, thou shalt be justified and by thy words thou shalt be condemned" (Matt 12:37) then become a reality. David ends up losing four of his own children to wicked circumstances, this baby, Amnon, Absalom, and Tamar. This baby died physically because of a parent's sin, which can be traced all the way back to the rebellion of Adam.

In the process of David's prayers of repentance and grief, the baby dies. David's profound words when asked about the child are, in 2 Samuel 12:23, "But now he is dead, wherefore should I fast? Can I bring him back again? I shall go to him, but he shall not return to me." David has the sure mercies and promise of God that he, himself, will be with God (Ps 23) and now has confidence that he will also see this child again.

The New Testament records the words of Jesus Christ concerning these infants when he states, in Luke 18:15–16, "And they brought unto him also infants, that he would touch them: but when *his* disciples saw *it*, they rebuked them. But Jesus called them *unto him*, and said, Suffer little children to come unto me, and forbid them not: for of such is the kingdom of God." These infants are said to be part of the kingdom of God as they are. Verse 17 of that same chapter states that one must accept the kingdom as a little child. That statement is aimed at adults who must simply "believe what God said." That is the faith of a child; they believe what they are told. Verse 15, however, specifies infants. These innocents are part of the kingdom of God as they are. They have not lost that privilege yet.

Job gives some insight into the salvation of infants as well. Job did say some things that God rebuked, as in the case of God using Elihu as his spokesman (Job 33:6), and then God's verbal rebuttal of Job's words (Job 38:1–2). God's chastisement of Job for Job's words was not about spiritual insight but Job's justification of himself. Those insights were not wrong and are never corrected in any place of Scripture.

Job mentions three times the spirituality of the unborn and newborn. The first of these is Job 3:11: "Why died I not from the womb? *Why* did I *not* give up the ghost when I came out of the belly?" Job declares his wish to be a stillborn baby. In that statement, he declares that he would give up the "ghost," the spirit. The interesting point is the usage of ghosts and their parallel to the New Testament usage of the Holy Spirit and Holy Ghost. The words are interchangeable, yet the remarkable point is that Holy Ghost is not used in the Old Testament. The reason for this is that a ghost is recognized as the spirit of a person who has died. Although the New Testament records the life of Jesus Christ, it is written after his death, burial, and resurrection. Hence, the Holy Ghost is the Spirit of the Lord, the third member of the Holy Trinity (1 John 5:7). Job is declaring his desire to have died before birth and yet recognizes he had a spirit at that time.

Job's second mention is Job 10:18: "Wherefore then hast thou brought me forth out of the womb? Oh, that I had given up the ghost, and no eye had seen me!" This statement is even more emphatic in Job's desire for his spirit to be taken to God while still in the womb, as stated, "and no eye had seen me." There seems to be no doubt in Job's mind about the fact that a child has a living spirit even though it is born of Adam. Adam's sin is the cause of death in all of mankind, but it is not the cause of the death of the spirit in mankind.

The Scriptures used to press the point of being born with a dead spirit are general statements made to an adult population. Ephesians 2:1 makes the statement "who were dead in trespasses and sins." The context of the verse must be noted in that Paul is addressing those who made a choice to accept Jesus as Christ, as also seen in the statement, "and you hath he quickened." Romans 3:23 gives the condemnation of mankind with "For all have sinned and come short of the glory of God." The wording of this passage must be noted in that "sinned" is a verb. It does not say that all "have sin," but that all have committed sin. This describes those who have made a choice to rebel against the righteousness of God in some way. Romans 5:12, as well as the other Scriptures used to prop the concept of original sin being spiritual death, can all be applied to the flesh within the context of their passages without changing any of the wording of the verses.

Job's third statement is Job 33:4: "The Spirit of God hath made me, and the breath of the Almighty hath given me life." God is still the creator and giver of life, even though that life is now in the blood (Lev 17:11). No life takes on reality without the giver of life being involved. A baby before birth is said to have a living spirit (Job 3:11; Job 10:18), a consciousness (Luke 1:41), recognition as a person by God (Ps 139:13), and a purpose (Jer 1:5). Not everyone has the purpose of the prophet Jeremiah, but every person has the purpose of giving Jesus Christ preeminence (Col 1:16–18). Job's declarations give abundant evidence of a baby having a living spirit. Jesus Christ confirms these Old Testament revelations when telling the disciples that the children are the kingdom of God (Luke 18:16).

The story of the gospels is the epic tale of how God is going to populate his kingdom. Every dispensation must have three elements: grace, faith, and obedience. The Old Testament required these, and yet the Israelites failed in their obedience. To remedy this sin, God sent forth his only begotten Son to be obedient to them. Yet this time, they failed in their faith. Goldingay states that many times people assume Jehovah to be wrathful and judgmental when a look at the specific time of Israel's spiritual need shows him to be a very merciful God.[2] Exodus 34:5–8 shows the reason for the incarnation of Jesus Christ. Although God could forgive sin, only the blood of the Lord Jesus Christ can clear sin away (Heb 9:12).

The purpose of this discourse on the kingdoms is to demonstrate that one cannot assume to apply the same quantifications to both kingdoms as they have different properties and requirements. Because a child is considered innocent or guilty in the kingdom of heaven will not necessarily have its equivalent in the kingdom of God. The Old Testament inheritance of the kingdom does not carry over to the New Testament covenant based upon birth by human DNA. Jesus is not declaring these infants to be part of the kingdom due to genetics, covenants, or rituals. The declaration of their inclusion is based upon their innocence, which is a living and unsoiled spirit.

There is a passage that has caused some, even evangelicals, to question the validity of an unborn child being recognized as a living soul and, thus, a living and innocent spirit. Exodus 21:22–23: "If men strive and hurt a woman with child so that her fruit depart *from her*, and yet no mischief follow: he shall be surely punished, according as the woman's husband will lay upon him; and he shall pay as the judges *determine*. And if *any* mischief follows, then thou shalt give life for life."

As seen in this passage, the word "fruit" is used to describe the unborn, and the punishment is one of monetary payment for causing the departure of that fruit. The argument would be that if this was a living person with a living spirit, then it would, of necessity under the law, be deemed a capital punishment crime.

Examining the passage for exactly what it says, though, will clear up the matter. Verse 22 clearly states that the woman is "with

2. Goldingay, *Israel's Faith*, 160.

child," not just with a mass of tissue or an undeveloped fetus. This statement places no restriction on the recognition of this child's development in the first, second, or third trimester of pregnancy. It is also noted that "no mischief follows." The causing of termination of the pregnancy is an unintentional act with no malice intended toward the woman or child. Verse 23 declares that if there is such malice aimed at the child, for whatever reason, then the punishment is "life for life."

To gain the mindset of this passage, it must be considered that Jewish Old Testament law mandates very specific rules regarding inheritances and birthrights. These rules may cause contention between men when one considers the brother's position of inheritance, as in the case of Esau and Jacob (Gen 25:31). These laws also affect the ownership of tribal lands, which must be returned in the Jubilee year (Lev 25:28). Boaz used these laws of inheritance to secure his marriage to Ruth the Moabitess (Ruth 4:6). Onan's sin of spilling his seed on the ground (Gen 38:9) is not an admonition against birth control or self-gratification but rather that of greed. Onan knew that the child he would produce with this widow of his brother would be considered in place of Onan's elder brother and would then have the birthright and the inheritance (Gen 38:8). Suffice it to say; these passages give ample reason to assume that mischief would be a very plausible motive for causing a woman to terminate her pregnancy and, thus, the severe penalty for purposely causing the death of this living unborn child.

The usage of the word "fruit" is of no real consequence as various terminologies are used for children. Jesus Christ, prophesied as the coming Messiah, is first mentioned in Gen 3:15 and referred to as "it." He is later described as that "holy thing" in Luke 1:35. Children are described as arrows in Ps 127:4–5.

There is no passage of Scripture that gives an indication of a baby being born with a dead spirit because of Adam's sin. Augustine's doctrine of original sin involving the spirit of a baby does not hold up under the spotlight of Scripture. It is generally accepted on the foundations of popular creed, tradition, and antiquity. The resulting doctrines of trying to wash away that infantile guilt also lack a scriptural foundation. There is no example of pedobaptism given in Scripture, nor is there any admonition to practice such. The need is totally based upon the acceptance of Augustine's concept of the guilty condition of a baby.

The tragedy is that even amongst Christians, the Scripture has become a non-authority

LOSS OF INNOCENCE

A child is born with Adam's sin upon them (Rom 5:12). That sin is contained in the body of flesh and is the reason for everyone's death, even that of an infant. There is a distinct difference between the death of the flesh and that of the spirit. The apostle Paul writes regarding this distinction in Rom 7:9: "For I was alive without the law once: but when the commandment came, sin revived, and I died." Paul's statement is that realizing the law of righteousness and consequently rebelling against it caused his death. He writes this passage as an adult and about himself. It is not a generic statement of mankind but a personal declaration of the cause of his own spiritual guilt and death.

Adam is a typology of all humanity. Humans are born with innocence before God, and sin is not imputed upon their spirits (Rom 5:13). Just like Adam, children are innocent even though they may have some knowledge of good and evil. A toddler will understand the command not to do something. That toddler will also understand there may be a punishment for disobedience. What he/she will not understand is that disobedience is a violation of the laws of universal righteousness, which God put in the heart of every cognitive adult (Rom 2:15).

If one is to accept the Augustinian view of original sin, then it is no great step to also accept taking away the responsibility of man's choices in regard to responsibility and ability.

The transgression of Adam gave all of mankind cursed flesh. This flesh is inclined to sin as; Paul states in Rom 7:18, "For I know that in me (that is, in my flesh) dwelleth no good thing: for to will is present with me, but *how* to perform that which is good I find not." His entire chapter of Rom 7 is one of bemoaning the sins of the flesh and the struggle against his born-again spirit. The flesh constantly battles against the spirit (Gal 5:17), which is not sinful. Regardless of whether that spirit is not sinful because it is born again in the Spirit of God (1 John 5:18) or if that spirit is sinless because it has not matured enough to understand the law of righteousness (Rom 5:13), the flesh still wages its war.

As a child grows, it will learn obedience and disobedience. Jesus Christ went through this same process of growth as he was manifest in the flesh born of a virgin (Heb 5:8). His learning of obedience would necessarily require his learning of disobedience. As Jesus grew, he was always able to keep his flesh in control and choose the right. By virtue of this choice, Jesus is our high priest who was tempted in all points, as is all of humanity, yet he was without sin (Heb 4:15).

This learning of obedience and disobedience matures into a learning of righteousness. God has placed upon the heart of every person to grow into a conscience of righteousness (Rom 2:15). This maturing then convicts the heart of not only a disobedient act and the consequential punishment but also of violating the universal law of what is righteous. This is why every society has some similar laws of conduct, as seen from the law of Moses to the Code of Hammurabi.

Some would try to place a particular age of accountability. The biblical passage used for this would be Luke 2:42. Jesus was twelve years old when he was found teaching in the temple. This has become the basis for some denominational confirmations taking place around the age of twelve. The concept is based upon tradition rather than Scripture.

The acquiring of accountability would be based more upon the environment of a child. One raised in a Christian home and growing up in a Bible-based church would naturally come to an understanding before one who was raised on the world's philosophies and rudiments. This knowledge of righteousness may come at different moments for people, but it does come to all who have the ability to mentally understand their conscience (John 1:9).

To violate this conscience, which is the guardian of the law of righteousness, is the line in the sand that would make a spirit guilty in the eyes of God. This negates the argument that one needs to leave the heathen alone since their lack of knowledge would be their salvation. Everyone is given that conscience of righteousness (Rom 2:15, John 1:9, Ps 19:1). What is not given is the plan of redemption for their spirits. That is the purpose of missionaries.

Regardless of whether they have ever heard the gospel, the name of Jesus, or seen a missionary, everyone stands in violation of their own conscience. The question is about their reaction to that conscience. Some would sear their conscience so it no longer speaks to them of righteousness and conviction (1 Tim 4:2). Others may look for the truth. As the will of God is explicitly stated to be that everyone would be saved (2 Pet 3:9), if someone wants truth God will get it to them. An example would be the Ethiopian eunuch of Acts 8. He is alone in the desert but seeking truth. God places Philip in his path in order for this man to get the truth for which he is longing. A missionary or evangelist may not always be available humanly speaking, but God will use whatever means necessary to reach someone who wants the truth; Heb 13:2: "Be not forgetful to entertain strangers: for thereby some have entertained angels unawares." For many, the final judgment of Rev 20 will be to answer how they reacted to the conviction from their conscience. When faced with their guilty conscience, did they try to find an answer? Did they seek something that was better than what they themselves were, or did they simply write their conviction off by assuming they were good enough? Their rejection of their convicted conscience is their rejection of righteousness. This rejection of conscience will then be their cause of suffering the condemnation of God.

A child is an heir to Adam's flesh and the sinfulness in that flesh. That child's spirit is only guilty upon his choosing to violate the laws of righteousness when he is able to understand those universal laws of conscience. The infant is not sin-stained in spirit. His spirit is clean and part of the kingdom of God until he makes a choice to sin against the righteousness of God and his conscience.

This is explained in scriptural detail in chapters four and five of this book.

Realizing these principles, it is extremely important to tread carefully in teaching and preaching to children. An adult with a charismatic personality may be able to guide a child into making a premature confession of faith without fully understanding the implications. Pedobaptism and these early confessions of faith have the same effect. When a child matures to that understanding of righteousness and their conscience convicts them of violating that righteousness, there is an impulse to rely on that infant baptism or immature reciting of a prayer for salvation. This causes much damage in trying to present the gospel to those who have the ability to understand, have been convicted by their conscience, and will still not yield to the righteousness of God.

Contemporary religion has become such a quantitative industry that they have sacrificed the souls of these innocents for the sake of numbers. Understanding the doctrines of scriptural infant innocence and the time of guilt allows one to prepare the ground for the seeds of the gospel to be planted (1 Cor 3:6).

The minister who will accept the scriptural doctrine of original sin rather than Augustine's version is able to have the utmost confidence in comforting parents who have suffered the loss of an innocent. They can also be comforted in the death of that person with the utmost assurance that these innocents are with the Lord. There need not be a lack of confidence by the minister, and with the full assurance of the Scripture, he is able to give a bold and clear presentation of God's grace in the death of these that are not accountable for sin. This would lend itself to an open door of witnessing for the grace of God. The minister may now present the mechanics of why that baby can be said to be saved, and the question remaining is whether the parents or loved ones will also accept the grace God provided for their salvation. As is often the case, God does not cause the tragedies, but he can use them to reach the hearts and lives of people who seek the truth.

A funeral can be said to be the time that Christians win. Psalms 116:15, "Precious in the sight of the LORD *is* the death of his saints." God did not save the saints for this life but for life to come, which is eternity. This confidence of where the saints and these innocents are at their time of death needs to be broadcast loud and clear (2 Corinthians 5:8). This is the basis of the statement that although Christians grieve at the temporary loss, it is not as if the world grieves because they have no hope. 1 Thessalonians 4:13 "But I would not have you to be ignorant, brethren, concerning them which are asleep, that ye sorrow not, even as others which have no hope."

Christians have the confident hope to know where they are going at the time of their earthly death (1 John 5:13) and to know where the souls of the innocents will be if one of them were to pass away (Romans 5:13)

Bibliography

Allison, Gregg. *Historical Theology.* Grand Rapids: Zondervan, 2011

———. *Sojourners and Strangers.* Wheaton, IL: Crossway, 2012.

"The Angel Moroni." Church of Jesus Christ of Latter-Day Saints. https://www. churchofjesuschrist.org/study/history/topics/angel-moroni?lang=eng.

Augustine. *Book of Confessions.* Translated by E. B. Pusey. London: J. M. Dent and Sons, 1957.

———. *St. Augustine's Confessions.* Translated by William Watts. London: William Heinemann Ltd., 1977.

———. *The Confessions of St. Augustine. Translated by Albert Cook Outler.* Mineola, NY: Dover Publications. Digitized format: https://archive.org/ details/isbn_9780486424668.

———. *The Anti-Pelagian Works.* Edinburgh: T & T., 1874.

———. *The City of God.* Translated by Gerald G. Walsh, et al. Garden City, NY: Doubleday Image, 1958.

Axworthy, Michael. "The Revenge of Pelagius." *New Statesman* 147.5448 (Dec 7, 2018) 18.

"Baptism for the Dead." Church of Jesus Christ of Latter-Day Saints. https:// newsroom.churchofjesuschrist.org/article/baptism-for-the-dead.

"Baptist Faith and Message 2000." https://bfm.sbc.net/bfm2000/.

Bauckham, Richard. "Universalism: A Historical Survey." *Themelios* 4.2. https:// www.thegospelcoalition.org/themelios/article/universalism-a-historical-survey.

Brown, Michel L. *Answering Jewish Objections to Jesus, Vol. 2.* Grand Rapids: Baker, 2000.

Butler, Brian H. "Infant Salvation: An Ecumenical Problem." *Foundations* 14.4 (Oct-Dec 1971) 344–60.

"By Water and the Spirit: A United Methodist Understanding of Baptism." United Methodist Church. https://www.umc.org/en/content/by-water-and-the-spirit-a-united-methodist-understanding-of-baptism.

Christensen, Michel M. "Original Sin from Justin Martyr to Augustine." https:// www.academia.edu/7832147/Original_Sin_from_Justin_Martyr_to_ Augustine.

Cohon, Samuel S. "Original Sin." *Hebrew Union College Annual* 21 (1948) 276–97.

Collins, C. John. "Adam and Eve in the Old Testament." *Southern Baptist Journal of Theology* 15.1 (Spring 2011) 4–25.

Couenhoven, Jesse. "Augustine's Doctrine of Original Sin." *Augustinian Studies* 36.2 (2005) 359–96.

Cyprian. *The Epistles of Cyprian*. Edinburgh: T. & T., 1868.

Eliade, Mircea. *A History of Religious Ideas, Vol. 3*. Translated by Alf Hiltebeitel and Diane Apostolos-Cappadona. Chicago: University of Chicago Press, 1985.

"FAQs about Doctrine." The Lutheran Church Missouri Synod. https://www.lcms.org/about/beliefs/faqs/doctrine.

Flowers, Leighton. "Theology II TH804." Trinity Biblical Seminary, On-Demand Webinar.

"The Formula of Concord ~ Solid Declaration." http://bookofconcord.org/sd-originalsin.php.

Freeman, Austin. "The Two Adams." MTh Theology in History, University of Edinburgh, August 17, 2012.

"General Council of Trent: Fifth Session." https://www.papalencyclicals.net/councils/trent/fifth-session.htm.

"General Council of Trent: Twenty-First Session." http://www.papalencyclicals.net/councils/trent/twenty-first-session.htm.

Gerrish, B. A. *Grace and Reason: A Study in the Theology of Luther*. Eugene, OR: Wipf and Stock, 1962

Gibson, David, and Jonathan Gibson. *From Heaven He Came and Sought Her*. Wheaton, IL: Crossway, 2013.

Goldingay, John. *Israel's Faith*. Old Testament Theology 2. Downers Grove, IL: InterVarsity, 2006

———. *Israel's Gospel*. Old Testament Theology 1. Downers Grove, IL: InterVarsity, 2003.

Hamilton, Alan H. "The Doctrine of Infant Salvation." *Bibliotheca Sacra* (July–September 1944) 470–82.

Harris, Paul R. "Civil Righteousness versus Civil Religion." *Logia* 15.3 (2006) 4.

Hawker, Sara, and Maurice Waite, eds. *Oxford Paperback Dictionary and Thesaurus*. https://archive.org/stream/paperbackoxforddoooounse#page/314/mode/2up.

Irenaeus. *Against Heresies*. https://archive.org/details/SaintIrenaeusAgainstHeresiesComplete/page/n313/mode/2up.

Jacobs, Louis. *Theology in the Responsa*. Portland: Littman Library of Jewish Civilization, 2005.

Jennings, David. *Pelagius: Defense of the Freedom of the Will*. http://www.seanmultimedia.com/Pie_Pelagius_Defense_Of_The_Freedom_Of_The_Will.html.

Justin Martyr. *Dialogue with Trypho*. Translated by Thomas B. Falls. Washington, D.C.: The Catholic University of America Press, 1965

Klaus Detlev Schulz. "Two Kinds of Righteousness and Moral Philosophy." *Concordia Biblical Quarterly* 73 (2009) 17–40.

Lopes Pereira, Jairzinho. *Augustine of Hippo and Martin Luther on Original Sin and Justification of the Sinner.* Gottingen: Vandenhoeck & Ruprecht, 2013.

Lumpkin, William L. *Baptist Confessions of Faith.* Philadelphia: Judson, 1959.

Luther, Martin. *The Jews and Their Lies.* Los Angeles: Christian Nationalist Crusade, 1948.

Melanchthon. *The Loci Communes of Philipp Melanchthon.* Translated by Charles Leander Hill. Boston: The Meador, 1944

Olsen, Daphne M. "Luther and Hitler: A Linear Connection between Martin Luther and Adolf Hitler's Anti-Semitism with a Nationalistic Foundation." https://scholarship.rollins.edu/mls/20/.

Origen. *The Writings.* Translated by Frederick Crombie. Edinburgh: T. & T., 1872.

———. "Origen's Writings." http://www.copticchurch.net/topics/patrology/schoolofalex2/chapter02.html.

Otto, Sean A. "Theism, Evil, and the Search for Answers: Some Recent Scholarship on Theodicy and the Problem of Evil." *Heythrop Journal* 56.1 (Jan 2015) 136–40.

The Oxford Dictionary of the Christian Church. Edited by F. L. Cross. Oxford: Oxford University Press, 1990.

The Oxford English Dictionary. Oxford: Oxford University Press, 2007

Paeth, Scott R. "Virtual Good and Evil." *The Christian Century* 129.6 (Mar 21, 2012) 22–25.

Phipps, William E. "The Heresiarch: Pelagius or Augustine?" *Anglican Biblical Review* 62.2 (Apr 1980) 124–33.

Rembaum, Joel E. "Medieval Jewish Criticism of the Christian Doctrine of Original Sin." *AJS Review* 7.8 (1982–83) 353–382.

Schaff, Philip. "On Marriage and Concupiscence." St. Augustine: Anti-Pelagian Writings. The Christian Classic Ethereal Library. Accessed July 2020. https://www.google.com/books/edition/_/Ympna9IBIIYC?hl=en&gbpv=1&bsq=conceived%20concupiscence.

Shedd, William G. T. *Dogmatic Theology.* Phillipsburg, NJ: P & R, 2003.

Shulz, Klaus Detlev. "Two Kinds of Righteousness and Moral Philosophy: *Confessio Augustana* XVIII, Philipp Melanchthon, and Martin Luther." *Concordia Biblical Quarterly* 73.1 (2009) 17–40.

Sorabji, Richard. *Emotion and Peace of Mind: From Stoic Agitation to Christian Temptation.* Oxford: Oxford University Press, 2000.

Tertullian. *On the Testimony of the Soul.* https://archive.org/details/tertullianontest00tertuoft/page/22.

"Thirty-Nine Articles of Religion." http://anglicansonline.org/basics/thirty-nine_articles.html.

The Unaltered Augsburg Confession, 1530 AD. Milwaukee, WI. Republished by Northwestern Pub. House. 2005. Accessed March 2020.

https://www.stpls.com/uploads/4/4/8/0/44802893/augsburg-confession. pdf.

Waldman, Nahum M. "What Was the Actual Effect of the Tree of Knowledge?" *Jewish Bible Quarterly* 19.2 (Winter 1990–91) 105–113.

Walton, John H., et al. *IVP Bible Backgrounds Commentary.* Downers Grove, IL: InterVarsity, 2000.

Weiss, Dov. "Sins of the Parents in Rabbinic and Early Christian Literature." *Journal of Religion* 97.1 (Jan 2017) 1–25.

Werblowsky, R. J. Zwi, and Geoffrey Wigoder. *The Encyclopedia of the Jewish Religion.* New York: Adama, 1986.

Wesley, John. "Original Sin." Edited by Thomas Jackson. https://web.archive. org/web/20180322103812/http://www.umcmission.org/Find-Resources/ John-Wesley-Sermons/Sermon-44-Original-Sin.

Wilder, William N. "Illumination and Investiture: The Royal Significance of the Tree of Wisdom in Genesis 3." *Westminster Biblical Journal* 68.1 (Spring 2006) 51–69.

Wilson, Ken. *The Foundation of Augustinian-Calvinism.* Montgomery, TX: Regula Fidei, 2019.